A Message from the Author

This is the 9th reprint of this *Best Selling* cultural book which over the years has become commonly known as

"The Fuchsia Bible"

It has earned this accolade because of its ability to explain, in simple terms, all aspects of fuchsia culture.

You will find my book refreshing in its style and content. It has only one theme and that is to tell you **"How to Grow Fuchsias"**. Each topic is explained in a detailed, easy to understand way. Nothing is left to the imagination.

The 15 chapters and 96 pages, dedicated entirely to fuchsia culture, are crammed full of tips and include many new ways of making it much easier to grow these marvellous plants. Perhaps the latest of my ideas, the Multi-Plant method, is the one that will benefit you the most.

This new technique means that *YOU* can grow beautiful flowering plants in less than half the time and without all the usual training. In fact *IT'S SO EASY IT'S ALMOST UNBELIEVABLE.*

Recommended by the National Gardening Press, Fuchsia Societies and Growers to their Friends.

"The Book is Simply the Best"

D0239105

Ken Pilkington

How to Grow Fuchsias
A Practical Guide
by Ken Pilkington
© 1997

First Published 1990
Revised edition published, February 1992
First reprint, May 1992
Second edition published, December 1992
First reprint of second edition, May 1993
Third edition published, June 1994
First reprint of third edition, June 1995
Second reprint of third edition, August 1996
Fourth edition published, September 1997

Published by Ken Pilkington, who also wishes to show appreciation to John Porter for his generosity in allowing the use of his photograph of the cultivar 'Margaret Pilkington' on the front cover.

Printed by: Forsyth & Steele, 161 Blackpool Old Road, Poulton-le-Fylde, Lancashire FY6 7RS.

Contents

Introduction

I thought I would begin by letting you know a little about myself and the history of the book before explaining how I grow my fuchsias. I have had almost a lifelong interest in gardening, beginning with helping my dad on his allotment. It continued after my marriage in 1964 and in fact it was Margaret who brought the first fuchsia home to join our collection of pot plants. At first I did not find them too easy to manage, but as I have always endeavoured to grow plants to their best I started to question the traditional, blanket, cultural advice given and began to amend it to better suit the rather un-fuchsia-like conditions of my south facing garden.

I gradually became more proficient and began to realise my simple approach to growing was being taken up, with success, by others to whom I passed on my tips. As I gained more confidence I began to put my knowledge down on paper and a set of cultural leaflets began to appear. These leaflets, with their *down to earth* advice, became so popular that it became impossible for me to keep up with producing them myself, so in 1990 they became the basis of the first edition of this book. Since that time "How to Grow Fuchsias" has been reprinted many times, each one fairly heavily revised as I learnt something new or improved my description of a certain point of culture.

In recent years I have developed a completely new approach to growing fuchsias, particularly for the bush and basket types of growth — I call it the Multi-Plant method. In many respects this new cultural procedure supersedes many older ways of growing but there is still a place for traditional methods, and learning about the different ways of growing fuchsias can only help you to have a more rounded view of their cultivation. This knowledge should then help you to evolve your own techniques in the search to master the growing conditions in the unique environment of your garden.

"How to Grow Fuchsias" now encompasses a cultural mixture of traditional methods, my adaptation of tradition, and also much that is modern, all or any of which can be used with the sure knowledge that they will give you success. Let me now describe, in the simplest terms that I can, exactly how I grow my fuchsias…

Growing Conditions

The conditions or environment in which we grow our plants are all important. You hear of so many people who say that they can't grow this or they can't grow that. They also say of someone who is successful with plants that they must have *'Green Fingers'*. Well, I think that anyone who has a mind to grow something could do so, if only they would take the trouble to find out how that particular plant thrives in its natural habitat. Then, to the best of their ability, reproduced a similar type of environment for their plants.

So, if *YOU* wish to be successful with fuchsias you now know that it is necessary to grow them in as near as possible the conditions found where they naturally grow. We can learn a lot by looking around us. If we do, we will notice fuchsias growing in gardens almost every day. We also will have seen them thriving in the hedgerows as we travel around. This should tell us something. The fuchsia is a shrub that does best in outdoor locations where the environment is cool, shady and humid.

Fuchsias, however, being perhaps the most versatile of plants, can be grown in pots or containers almost anywhere as long as you provide the conditions that best suit them. Let me begin this most important aspect of fuchsia culture by considering the above three cultural points and explain how I create the *CORRECT* growing conditions in perhaps the hardest environment to control, the small greenhouse.

Note: If you do not have a greenhouse, use the following as a guide for the conditions required wherever you grow your plants.

Ventilation: Keeping the small greenhouse cool in summer is not easy to achieve. Most manufacturers simply do not provide sufficient ventilation to give the changes of air required to keep summer temperatures at the lowest possible level. My answer to the problem is to remove (from early June) some panes of glass or base panels from low down on the sides and end of my 12 foot by 8 foot greenhouse (two on each side and two at the end). I support glass that may slip with wooden dowelling and cover the open spaces with fine mesh plastic netting to keep out unwelcome Birds, Bees, Wasps, etc. I also remove the panes at the apex of each gable end as these make invaluable extra roof vents — all glass is, of course, replaced in the autumn.

Note: I now create an even better ventilating system, in conjunction with the above, in my small greenhouse during the summer months. I have found that it is quite easy to lower the top row of glass on each of the walls and also the gable end. I remove the retaining clips and slide each pane down about 2 or 3 inches and refit sufficient clips to hold the glass firmly in place. The gap is then covered with plastic mesh to keep pests out. The resultant throughflow of air in the greenhouse keeps the temperature much lower and the plants more comfortable. If it is not possible to lower glass on your greenhouse it may will be worth your while to buy several pieces of glass cut a little shorter, these can then be used in place of the original ones.

A netted wooden frame replaces the door and, except in high winds, the roof vents kept wide open. Taking these measures mean that warm air escaping through the upper vents is replaced by cool air entering through the lower ones, thus ensuring good air circulation and a much cooler greenhouse.

Two further points of interest are;

• A common piece of equipment for the small amateur greenhouse is the automatic vent opener. These can be extremely useful in the early part of the year, especially if you have to leave home early on frosty mornings. My only reservation on these is that they open far too late for my liking on the hot days of summer, they also close far too early. My advice is to disconnect them for the summer months, fastening the open windows firmly down onto suitable lengths of wooden dowelling to prevent wind damage.

• One of the problems of flowering pot grown fuchsias in the greenhouse in summer is that the flowers on some cultivars open badly marked. The reason for this is that the bud, prior to it opening, contains a great deal of moisture. This, on a hot day can create a STEAMY atmosphere inside the bud, so much so that it virtually scalds the delicate tissues of the flower. All the more reason to keep the greenhouse as cool as possible on hot days.

Shade: No one can tell you exactly how much to shade your greenhouse. The amount needed will depend on the aspect of your garden, which direction it faces and how much shade it gets from fences, trees, etc. It can also depend in which part of the country you reside. If you live in an area with a clear atmosphere you will probably need more shading than someone who lives near industry, because pollution arising from an industrial area will, to some extent, filter the sun.

I can start, depending on the weather, to shade my greenhouse as early as late February, giving the glass a light coating of 'Coolglass', a white shading material that is painted on the glass. February may seem early, but it is surprising how strong the sun can be at that time of year, particularly through the glass of a small greenhouse. Do not forget it is also about then that overwintered plants are starting to show signs of life, and that their delicate new leaves and shoots can easily be damaged by sun. The seasons early cuttings could also be in their first stages of growth, these also need the protection of light shade. This first application is usually sufficient until early May, then I apply a thicker coat of shading for the brighter sun of summer.

Humidity: Many plants, and fuchsias in particular, do not grow well in a dry atmosphere. The usual advice given for creating humidity is to spray around the plants with water and wet the floor of the greenhouse on the mornings of bright days. This is all well and good whilst moisture remains, but after a couple of hours on a sunny day it may well have evaporated to leave a dry atmosphere again.

You can improve the situation quite simply. My way of overcoming the problem is to raise the edge of the staging by about an inch and cover the entire area of the staging with a sheet of heavy gauge polythene. I then fill the resultant reservoir to a depth of about three quarters of an inch with any moisture retaining material. The one I favour is grit graded to one eighth (3mm) of an inch in size. The beauty of grit is that the surface dries out under sun and discourages the growth of algae, which although it does no harm can be a bit of a mess.

Beginning in late February, I spray water between the plants early on sunny days. This should ideally dry out by nightfall as it is unwise to have too much moisture lying about at that time of year. I progressively use more water as the days grow warmer, and from May onwards keep the benches permanently wet for the rest of the summer. Two points to note are:

- Do not have the benches so wet that plant pots are stood in water.
- If you find that plants are taking up water from the benches by capillary action, either use less water or place them on saucers.

These are the methods I use to combat the conditions in the *SOUTH* facing, extremely sunny (when the sun is out that is) garden of my home in Poulton-le-Fylde (about 2 miles inland from the sea at Blackpool). It will be up to you to adapt them to suit your own environment.

Remember, no matter where you grow your fuchsias the growing conditions should provide plenty of fresh air, an abundance of humidity, and some shade.

Metric Conversions

I have used imperial measurements throughout the book simply because, as a grower of more than a few years experience, I still think in inches where pot sizes are concerned. However, as most pots these days are marked in metric I think it may be of help if I give you the approximate conversions.

2" = 5cm: 2½" = 6cm: 3" = 8cm 3½" = 9cm: 4" = 10cm:

4¼" = 11cm: 5" = 13cm: 6" = 15cm: 7" = 18cm.

The above information relates mainly to standard 'full' (approximately as high as the top is wide) plant pots which have a distinct taper from top to bottom. Pots in the above sizes can usually also be obtained in different depths or heights.

As well as the standard shaped pot the black commercial 'shrub' pots can usually be obtained from Garden Centres or Nurseries. These pots tend to have a less tapered wall and are usually marked with the amount of compost that they hold, usually in litres. The main sizes that I tend to use are 1, 2, 3, and 4 litres, and their approximate metric and imperial measurements are as follows:

1 litre = 13cm or 5": 2 litre = 17cm or 6½": 3 litre = 19cm or 7½":

4 litre = 21cm or 8¼".

Suitable Composts

When we begin to grow fuchsias in pots or any other type of container I don't think many of us realise just how much skill it will take to keep them in good health, not only for a few weeks or months, but quite possibly for several years. To grow a fuchsia to its full potential in a relatively small amount of compost does need a certain amount of skill. There is one thing, however, that will help us to achieve our aim and that is the use of a well drained, aerated and nutritious compost.

I will now describe several types of compost you can buy, or that you can make up yourself. Each one is excellent for use in pots, but one of them may be better than the others for your plants in the environment in which you are growing them. It will be up to you to try them out and find which one gives you the best results.

Note: The compost that I would advise MOST *growers, especially beginners, to use is one made from the last recipe at the end of this chapter, the one which uses a bought multi-purpose potting compost. This interestingly enough is the compost I used when I started growing fuchsias and is the one that I have returned to after my experiments with other types. The reason? It suits* MY *plants, in* MY *garden, best.*

The main types of compost are:

Soil Based: This is usually made to the John Innes formula and comes in three strengths. I have used No.1 strength, which has 4ozs. of base fertiliser to the bushel (eight gallons of compost equals one bushel) for rooted cuttings and pots up to the 3" size. John Innes No.2, which contains 8ozs. of base fertiliser, for pots between 3½" and 6" in size. I would only use John Innes No.3, 12ozs. to the bushel for very vigorous cultivars in large containers.

My only reservation about using soil based composts is that good quality loam, which is their main ingredient, is no longer readily available. They also have a short shelf life, although if Vitax Q4 is used as the base fertiliser that time will be lengthened. Having said that, if you can obtain a supply that is fresh and of consistent high quality, then this is still a very good compost to use for your larger pots of fuchsias.

Note: I would not use any soil based compost for potting up very young plants.

Soilless Multi-Purpose Potting Compost: This type of compost is usually based on peat and has several points in its favour. It is light, clean, easy to use and because of these good points is probably the compost most commonly used. However, although containing all the nutrients necessary for growth, to my mind it has one fault with regard to its use in pots, particularly for plants like fuchsias that will be living in a pot for a long period of time. The fault that I am talking about is actually one of its best attributes, its ability to take up and retain moisture. Pot plants growing solely in multi-purpose compost need a great deal more care with watering. It is so easy to water plants without looking to see if they need watering or not. Anyone keeping a plant with the compost in a permanently wet state will almost certainly lose that plant, because the roots will have lost their essential supply of oxygen. Changes of air in a pot are equally as important as changes of air in a greenhouse. Compost *SHOULD* be allowed to go towards the dry side (not wilting) before rewatering, thus giving regular changes of air to the roots.

Roots that do not get regular changes of air soon rot and die.

The problem of careful watering can be greatly eased and pot plants more easy to manage if some additional materials are incorporated into the compost. My mix always includes 25% of aerating and drainage materials to 75% of soilless compost.

Note: I will explain which materials I use later in the chapter.

Alternative Soilless Compost: This type of compost is made from Coconut Fibre or some other alternative to peat. I have not been tempted to use any of these composts as yet because I do not believe that at present they compare to a good quality peat based soilless compost. I am quite sure that sometime in the future someone will come along with an alternative product that will at least be as good as one based on peat. In the meanwhile, because growing a plant in a pot is difficult enough as it is, I will continue to use something that I know will give me success over the long periods of time that I keep most of my pot plants. Let me stress that this is a *PERSONAL* view and I am not attempting to put you off using them. What I would suggest, however, is that you treat this type of compost like any other that you are trying for the first time, and only grow

6

a few plants in it to start with until you are sure that it gives you satisfactory results.

As you get more proficient at growing fuchsias you may wish to experiment with your cultural methods, with the aim of finding which type of compost or feed suits YOUR plants best in the environment of YOUR garden. To achieve this you may perhaps want to make up a compost of your own. One that, because you know exactly what it contains, will give you more control over growth. One of the benefits of making your own compost is that, because you only make as much as you need, it is always fresh. The quality is always excellent because you choose only the best materials, and as you always measure and mix them carefully the results are constant. I will now describe the ingredients needed to make a good quality soilless compost.

Note: I would recommend, or even stress, that all beginners should start by using a peat based multi-purpose potting compost (see last compost recipe on page 11). I would also recommend that ALL very young plants, especially in the early part of the year, should be potted up in the same type of compost.

Peat: This is the major part of the compost and should be SPHAGNUM moss peat (commonly called Irish moss peat) which is light brown in colour. Do NOT use sedge peat, which is black or blended peat which is a mixture of the two. In my opinion these are really only suitable for the garden.

Horticultural Grit is necessary for good drainage. It also adds weight to the pot, helping to make large plants more stable. The grading of the grit is important, if it is too fine the compost will become compacted, will not retain enough aeration, and will probably lead to waterlogging of the roots. If you use a grit that is too large the compost will be too open, allowing water to drain away too freely and with it the leaching of plant foods. The ideal seems to be a grit or very coarse sand, ideally graded at about one eighth of an inch (3mm). I use horticultural grit, but a coarse washed river sand (from the builder's yard or garden centre) will serve the same purpose. The fine sand used for bricklaying or sand from the beach should NOT be used. Grit also plays another important role in the compost, roots that would normally grow directly towards the warmth at the wall of the pot, are continually being deflected by particles of grit into other areas of the compost. This helps to make a better root system and more use of nutrients.

Perlite is an inert volcanic product that I always use in my compost. Here are some of its many useful qualities:

- It keeps the compost open, helping to keep air around the roots.
- It holds a tremendous amount of moisture, yet allows excess water to drain from the pot.
- It allows you to firm the compost without it becoming compacted.
- It helps to overcome the worst feature of soilless composts, and that is their tendency to shrink away from the wall of the pot if the compost becomes dry. This makes them extremely difficult to moisten as water tends to run down between compost and pot. With the inclusion of perlite in the compost, however, shrinkage is almost eliminated and water immediately taken up, so easing the problem of rewatering.

Note: Vermiculite has similar qualities to perlite and can be used in its place but there is one point that I would like you to be aware of: perlite is hard — vermiculite is soft. I have found that peat based composts with perlite and grit added can be firmed (just gently with young plants but quite heavily with older plants in 5" or larger pots but as I have no experience with vermiculite it will be up to you to experiment and see if the fact that it is soft makes any difference.

One thing that I am quite sure of is that all plants would prefer to feel that their roots have a secure hold in the compost and that a puff of wind would not blow them over. Some good points that occur if you do firm the compost are: a) Perlite does not float to the top when watered. b) Water does not evaporate anywhere near as quickly, even my 3½" pots invariably only need watering once a day. c) The cane used to support a Standard does not fall over.

I have always thought it strange that you wouldn't dream of NOT firming a plant in when planting it in the garden, yet the same plant would be just loosely potted up with perhaps a tap on the bench to settle it in if placed in a pot.

Because peat, horticultural grit and perlite have no food value, it is now necessary to add the bits and pieces that will give the plant something to feed on. A good compost will require in varying ratios:

Nitrogen: Plants need Nitrogen for vegetative growth, to feed leaves, stems, etc. and to build up the plants structure.

Phosphates are needed for root development and are most important, for without a good root system a plant will never reach its full potential.

Potash: This element enhances flower colour and helps to ripen growth.

Trace Elements: These are just as important to the plant as nitrogen, phosphates and potash. It is essential that the compost contains all the trace elements necessary for plant growth. In a soil based compost they are naturally present in the loam, but in a soilless one they have to be added.

The six main trace elements are Magnesium, Iron, Manganese, Copper, Boron and Molybdenum. They are often included in minute quantities, for example, one of the base fertilisers that I have used included Molybdenum at the rate of one part per million. This small amount may seem ridiculous but without it plants could suffer from a deficiency of this element.

Lime: This is necessary to sweeten the acidity of the peat to a point that is suitable for the plants and is known as the pH level of the compost. In my experience fuchsias will grow and thrive in composts that have a wide range of pH levels, so they are something that I don't bother about too much. However, my advice to help you get the pH level reasonably right when making compost is:

- Always use a good quality *SPHAGNUM* moss peat.
- Use horticultural grit or coarse sand with a neutral pH
- Add only the amount of lime recommended by the manufacturer of the base fertiliser.

Note: It is important that you use a lime that is suitable for use in potting composts. Do NOT use hydrated or garden lime as they are far too strong and will burn the roots. There are two types of lime that I use:

Dolomite Lime is excellent as it also contains the trace element Magnesium. My only criticism is that, because it is usually obtained in dust form, it can be easily leached from the compost.

Ground Limestone is also a good lime to use and as it is usually coarser ground than Dolomite lime tends to last much longer in the compost.

Calcified Seaweed can also be used to sweeten compost as 50% of its make up is Calcium. Calcified seaweed is organic and contains all the natural trace elements. It is recommended for use in place of, or as well as, lime and its inclusion will improve plant vigour and flower colour.

As most people only require small amounts of compost at any one time I will give the quantities to make up one gallon. Simply multiply the quantities if larger amounts are needed. A gallon of compost is easily made by following these three simple stages:

- Measure out the peat, horticultural grit (or coarse sand) and perlite by volume, not weight — *I use an old kitchen measuring jug.*

- Accurately weigh the base fertiliser, calcified seaweed, and lime if it is needed for the compost.

- Place everything in a large plastic bag and close the neck. Now, take hold of the bag at each end and tip it up and down so that the contents spill from end to end. After about 10 times the compost will be thoroughly mixed. *Note: Let it stand for a few days before using.*

Listed below are the composts that I have used in my search for the one that suits plants best, in *MY* garden. I can recommend all of them, but like me you may find one of them better than the rest for plants growing in *YOUR* garden.

Soilless compost using Vitax Q4 base fertiliser.

COMPOST No. 1 — Use for rooted cuttings and pots up to 3".

6 pints sphagnum moss peat.
1 pint horticultural grit.
1 pint perlite.
½ oz Vitax Q4.
½ oz lime.
½ oz calcified seaweed.

COMPOST No. 2 — Use for 3½" to 6" pots.

6 pints sphagnum moss peat.
1 pint horticultural grit.
1 pint perlite.
1 oz Vitax Q4.
½ oz lime.
½ oz calcified seaweed.

COMPOST No.3 — Use for 7" pots upwards.

6 pints sphagnum moss peat.
1 pint horticultural grit.
1 pint perlite.
1¼ oz Vitax Q4.
½ oz lime.
½ oz calcified seaweed.

Note: One thing to be aware of is that composts made with Vitax Q4 as the base fertiliser work best with temperatures at or above 50° Fahrenheit. I would recommend that these composts are better used in the summer months.

Soilless compost using Chempak potting base.

6 pints sphagnum moss peat.
1 pint horticultural grit.
1 pint perlite.
1¾ oz of Chempak potting base.

Notes on Chempak Potting Compost:

- Do *NOT* add lime to Chempak potting base, it is already included.

- In case of a change of packaging it would be advisable to weigh the contents and divide the weight by the number of gallons of compost the manufacturer states the pack will make. The result will be the amount of potting base to use to make one gallon of compost.

- If you use only small quantities of Potting Base at any one time, keep the remainder in a plastic storage box and shake to mix the ingredients before making the next batch of compost.

To make a peat based multi-purpose soilless potting compost suitable for container grown plants use:

6 measures of multi-purpose compost.
1 measure of horticultural grit.
1 measure of perlite.

Some notes on the above compost are:

- I have no preference as to which make of multi-purpose potting compost I buy, whether it is made by Levington, Arthur Bowers or any other manufacturer. The requirement I must have, however, is that the compost is based on sphagnum (Irish) moss peat. I use the fact that this type of peat fades in colour as it dries out as a sign not only whether a particular plant needs watering, but also as a guide as to how much water to give that plant. Composts made from sedge peat, the black stuff, do not fade in colour and give you no visual sign as to when to water a plant.

- This compost can be used immediately.
- The above measure can be any size you wish as long as you use the same one for each ingredient.
- You can add calcified seaweed (its use is optional) at the rate of half an ounce per gallon of compost.
- Adding perlite and grit will reduce the food value of the compost by a quarter but don't worry, just start liquid feeding your plants a couple of weeks earlier than the manufacturer recommends.
- This is the compost that I use for propagating cuttings in my Multi-Plant methods.

Résumé: These first two chapters have covered what I call the basic conditions for growing fuchsias in pots or containers. If your plants do not thrive you can bet your bottom dollar that either the conditions for good growth have not been provided or you have used a poor compost.

I make no apologies for emphasising once again that fuchsias require:

- **Plenty of fresh air.**
- **Humidity in abundance during the summer months.**
- **Shade and feed as required in the environment of your home or garden.**
- **And a decent compost in which to grow.**

Having put everything in place for good quality growth we can now start to grow our plants, and that of course begins with propagation...

Propagation

We now come to my favourite part of gardening, propagation. No matter how often I sow seeds or take cuttings I never lose the fascination of seeing young plants taking on a life of their own. The fact that fuchsias are so easy to propagate is probably the main reason why they are so popular, and in my case an obsession.

Although fuchsias can be raised from seed, it is only some of the Fuchsia Species that come true to type. Seed taken from any hybrid will grow into an entirely new cultivar with its own characteristics. It will then have to be propagated by vegetative means (cuttings) if you wish to multiply your stock from that particular cultivar.

Let us now consider the gentle art of raising fuchsias from cuttings. I take two types of cutting. Firstly, those obtained from the type of soft growth that appears on plants in spring, which I will describe under the heading *SPRING* cuttings. The second type is taken during the summer months from plants that are coming into bud or even flowering, these I will call *SEMI-RIPE* cuttings.

Spring Cuttings: To start with we have to decide how we are going to root them. Many people root their cuttings by placing them in water, or even in the rooting gels which are occasionally seen for sale in Garden Centres. I do not advocate either of these methods because the roots that emerge are water roots. This type of root is very brittle and easily broken, also, being a root that has been developed to take up nutrients from liquid, it is not of much use to the young plant when it is first potted up. Indeed, it could even receive a check in growth whilst it develops the type of root system that will enable it to take up food from compost. I believe that you get far better results by rooting them in a suitable compost. With the advent of my Multi-Plant method (see next chapter) I now use two different composts, dependant on how I intend to grow on my plants.

The two composts are:

Cutting Compost: I use this compost (described on page 15) only for plants that I will be pricking out to make up Multi-Plants or potting up as single plants.

Potting Compost: The majority of my Multi-Plants are now rooted in the same compost I use for potting up my plants (multi-purpose compost recipe on page 11). I will explain this method of starting fuchsias into growth later.

Having chosen the compost, all that remains is to decide where to place the cuttings so that they are in the right conditions for them to root. What are these right conditions you ask? Well, let me explain. As we are going to cut off the young shoots supply of life giving sap when we remove it from its mother plant we have, in some way, to place it where it will not dehydrate. You can adapt many household objects for this purpose. For example, an inverted coffee jar makes a perfect small propagator. Place a small pot (if you cut the rim off a 2½" plastic pot it fits inside a 200 gram coffee jar) of cuttings on the upturned lid (remove the sealing disc), screw on the jar, (they do not need ventilation), and you have the perfect conditions for cuttings whilst they develop roots.

Many other throw away objects (they must have a clear top) that once contained food, e.g. Cress Boxes also make ideal propagators. In fact the only purpose made propagator that I use is the 8½" by 6" unheated propagator which is easily obtained from most Garden Centres. The thing in common with all these propagators is that they allow cuttings to live in their own micro-climate of high humidity. So whether you have a heated greenhouse or just a windowsill in the home, you can take and strike cuttings successfully.

Note 1: I no longer use bottom heat to root cuttings. It takes a little longer to root them in the gentle warmth of the greenhouse or home, but you will find that if you place them in cool conditions they will make much sturdier, healthier plants. I have even rooted some in a coffee jar propagator during the winter in a cold greenhouse — just covering it with horticultural fleece on the very cold nights.

Note 2: If you do use a heated propagator, especially the small manufactured ones for the home, take care that the temperature of the compost gets no higher then 65° Fahrenheit. Excessive heat does two things: a) It causes growth to be weak and elongated. b) It also causes far too much humidity to be created, and an excess of humidity is one of the reasons why cuttings are lost.

Note 3: I have a theory that there is a relationship between the area of moist compost and the volume of air in the propagator. The 200 gram coffee jar with its 2½" pot makes a perfect propagator, as also does the 8½" by 6" covered tray. It seems a strange thing to me that I can get 100% success time after time when I use the 8½" by 6" propagator, yet I have never achieved anywhere near that percentage in the 14" by 8" propagator. My simple reasoning can only come up with the answer that the area of moist compost in the larger tray does not balance with the volume of air in the cover quite as well as the smaller one. I only mention this because it interests me and perhaps there is something from it that we can learn.

Having decided on the propagator that you are going to use let's leave it for the present and let me take you through my adaptation of the traditional (50% peat – 50% sharp sand) cutting compost. To make a perfect medium for rooting cuttings in trays you should use:

Two Parts Sphagnum Moss Peat: Peat, although it has no food value is perfectly all right to use for cuttings, but the young plants must be moved into a compost containing nutrients soon after they have rooted. If you would prefer to have some food in your cutting compost you can, of course, use a multipurpose soilless compost instead of peat.

Note: I always used peat when I was growing plants for the showbench because I found that growth was more short jointed than when I used multi-purpose compost.

One Part Sharp Sand: Horticultural sharp sand, or coarse washed river sand is the type to use. Do *NOT* use fine brick laying sand.

One Part Perlite: This is a most important, if not vital, ingredient. It helps to keep the compost open and aerated (very important). It is free draining, yet holds a tremendous amount of water. It keeps the compost evenly moist and is a great aid to rooting.

Note: Vermiculite has similar qualities.

Having mixed the compost I moisten it before filling the container. This allows me to get the moisture content just right. Taking the amount of compost that I need, I gently add water and mix it in until it reaches the stage when, if squeezed fairly hard, water just does *NOT* drip. If it becomes too wet and water does drip, simply add some dry compost until it reaches the required state. Leave it to settle for a little while before loosely filling the container, give it a light tap to settle the compost and top it up again. Level off the surface (do *NOT* firm) and you are ready to take your cuttings.

The advice mostly heard about the type of cutting to take is that it should have several sets of leaves and measure one or two inches in length. However, the method I use and would strongly advise you to try uses only the soft growing tip of the shoot. My reasons for using tip cuttings instead of longer ones are:

- Growth is much softer.

- They root much quicker, and more evenly.

- The most important point is that sideshoots emerge much lower down the stem, often from compost level, thus making a better plant.

My cutting usually comprises of the tiny growing point plus the first pair of leaves, two pairs if it is a short jointed cultivar. To give you some idea of the size of the cutting, the pieces of material I use are basically the tiny pieces removed when stopping or pinching out a plant.

Taking the plant (*MAKE CERTAIN THAT IT IS NOT WILTING*) from which I wish to propagate, I carefully look for a strong growing shoot, one with leaves that are of even size (even leaves usually lead to even growth) on each side of the growing tip. I also look down the stem at the young sideshoots emerging from the leaf axils, these also should be of equal size. Having chosen the shoot, I take a sharp knife (do *NOT* use your thumb nail or scissors as these will crush and bruise the stem) and cut it from the plant just above the pair of leaves immediately below the cutting. I then trim off the stem of the cutting to leave about an eighth of an inch (not too close) below the lower leaves.

Note: The even cutting mentioned above is important if you are growing a single plant in a pot, but it is not as important when using the Multi-Plant method (fully covered later in the book) when almost any tip will do.

Before going further I think you should know that Botrytis (Grey Mould) is the greatest enemy of the cutting, so there are several points that I would like you to be aware of:

- You *SHOULD NOT* allow leaves to lie on wet compost or to touch the leaves of other cuttings.

- Most importantly you *MUST NOT* allow your cuttings to wilt. If you have lost cuttings in the past, it is quite likely that they wilted at some stage. Cuttings can also be lost from Botrytis if there is too much humidity in the propagator. Too large an area of moist compost or too much heat can cause this problem.

- Having mentioned wilting it is most important that the shoots of the plant you going to propagate from arc fully turgid. It would be wise, if you are not quite sure, to give all your mother plants some water a few hours before taking cuttings.

My method of avoiding the problem of wilting is to trim the larger leaves of the cutting (to reduce transpiration), to leave just a tiny portion of the leaf on its stalk. Do not remove all of the leaf as you may damage the embryo sideshoots in the leaf axils. I also remove the tips of the leaves nearest the top of the cutting. The growing tip, which is hidden between those leaves is, of course, *NOT* touched. You are now left with what is, especially the first time you try this method, something that I know looks more than slightly ridiculous, but I can assure you that it works and is a highly successful way of taking cuttings. To give you another guide as to how small they are, I can comfortably get 7 cuttings around the edge of a 2½" pot and 54 (9 rows of 6) in the 8½" x 6" propagator without them being anywhere near touching.

Now, take the prepared cuttings lightly between finger and thumb and insert them (there is no need to soak them in fungicide or to use rooting powder) into the top surface of the compost. All that you are doing is standing them upright. Give them a light mist of water, label them and put the cover on the propagator, keeping the vent closed. Kept in a cool, shady place and not disturbed the cuttings will root in their own time, about three weeks at 65° Fahrenheit, longer at lower temperatures. You will see through the sides of the cover when rooting takes place because the leaves on the cuttings start to freshen up and begin to show a brighter colour.

Note: A better description of where to place, and what to look out for, whilst cuttings are rooting is given in the second point on page 24.

I do not advocate potting up rooted cuttings directly from the high humidity of the propagator. Doing this and placing them in the much drier atmosphere of the greenhouse or home could cause a check in growth, so some means must be found to harden them off. The coffee jar, for example, could have two small pieces of split cane placed across the lid (on each side of the pot) with the jar resting on them, leaving it like that for about a week before removing it altogether. I harden off rooted cuttings in the small propagator in different ways, depending on how I am going to grow the plants:

Note: I mentioned a 'check in growth' in the last paragraph and thought a few more words on the subject wouldn't harm. A check in growth is my own term for a cultural problem that occurs on very young plants, and is something that most of us will have experienced at some stage or another after buying in plants from Nurseries, Garden Centres or even on plants we have raised ourselves. The signs of the problem are fresh green leaves prematurely falling of the plant and, on inspection, the stem of the young plant prematurely ageing and turning woody.

In the majority of cases plants that develop this problem do not survive, but do not throw them out straight away as there are two things that you may be able to do: a) Take cuttings if there are any fresh shoots available. b) Keep an eye on the woody stem, sometimes the bark will start to show cracks — if this happens the plant has a good chance of recovering.

There is not a lot that you can do to prevent the problem happening on plants that you have bought or have been given because the fault probably happened before they came into your possession. But if it happens on plants you have raised yourself a check in growth has been caused by not hardening them off properly — see above and in the next paragraph.

Method One: If the plants are going to be grown on individually I fill a 14" by 8½" propagator with potting compost. I then prick out the rooted cuttings, spacing them out so that they have room to develop. By replacing the cover, with the vents closed, the young plants are back in high humidity. After a few days I open the vents to lower the humidity level. After another few days I prop up one end of the cover by about a quarter of an inch to allow air to circulate. A few days later I remove the cover altogether. The plants have now become hardened off to the conditions in which they are to grow. I now allow them to develop until the leaves are nearly touching, then pot them on into 2" or 2½" pots and grow them on as described in the chapters on Bushes and Standards.

Note 1: Pricking plants out into a tray of compost instead of straight into pots produces a much better root system.

Note 2: If you have used a heated propagator to aid rooting do NOT replace the tray on heat after pricking out the young plants.

Method Two: If the 'Multi-Plant' Method (see next chapter) is going to be used it is better to harden the young plants off, as described above, in the propagator in which they were rooted as the plants need to be moved on before the root gets too large.

Below is a list of Do's and Don'ts to note when using this method of taking cuttings:

- Do include perlite or vermiculite in your cutting compost.

- Do place cuttings in the compost immediately you have taken them, mist and label them, then replace the cover with the vents closed.

- Do shade from sunlight. Ideally, in good light but out of sun altogether.

- Do use soft, fresh growth for your cuttings, the type that naturally occurs in spring is ideal.

- Do not allow the temperature of the compost in the tray to get too high.

- Do not let the compost dry out. If you moistened the compost as previously described you shouldn't have to water it again during the rooting period. If you do need to re-water, do so as described for watering Multi-Plants on page 25.

- Do not remove the cover unnecessarily.

- Do not remove the cover to wipe off condensation, or to remist the cuttings.

Finally, remember that although the length of cutting you take doesn't matter, what does matter are the conditions in which you place them. They should provide *High Humidity with Shade*.

Semi-Ripe Cuttings: When I first started to recommend this method of taking cuttings it was mainly for autumn use, as an insurance against losing older plants in winter. Since then, however, I have used it more and more during the summer months for rooting shoots that are either just coming into bud or are in the early stages of flowering. I know that taking cuttings from flowering plants is opposed to most advice given, so here are my reasons for doing so:

- For the purpose we want them for it doesn't matter a jot that they are in bud or flower when we take them, because they will grow through the flowering stage as the daylight length of autumn and early winter shortens.

- Summer is the best time to take cuttings for growing on as Standards. My reason for saying this is that in my sunny garden spring cuttings start flowering long before they get tall enough for me to begin developing the head. By taking cuttings in late June, the whole of July and August or even early September you can have beautiful flowering Standards, with 10" to 15" stems, the following summer.

- Summer is also the time when we should be thinking of producing cutting material for early the following year (see below).

Rooting semi-ripe growth is not quite as easy as cuttings taken from the soft growth of spring. In fact I found that when I used a cutting compost to root them the results were very poor. There is one way, however, that I have found very successful and that is to root them in water, but with a difference. Take any type of container (I use a 4¼" half plant pot lined with a suitably sized polythene freezer bag, but a similar sized empty margarine container would also do) and fill it with either perlite or vermiculite. Now pour water into the container until it is filled to the top.

Since devising this method of propagating semi-ripe cuttings (it works equally well with many other varieties of plant) I have amended it several times. I would now suggest that you use shoots about 2" long, they should have the growing tip plus two pairs of leaves, and that are perhaps just in bud, as opposed to being in full flower (still take them even if they are in full flower). Trim the cutting below the bottom pair of leaves to leave just over quarter of an inch of stalk, then remove any buds (and flowers if there are any) that are large enough to handle. Reduce the leaf area if quite large and insert each cutting, after first making a hole in the perlite with a piece of split cane, down to the first pair of leaves.

Take your cuttings in numbers of at least 10 and preferably 14 or 15, then place 8 or 9 around the edge of the pot so that they are not touching one another, then fill in the centre with the remainder. Place them in a well lit but not sunny position (they should not be allowed to wilt) and do *NOT* cover them as you would cuttings in compost. Depending on the temperature they can root in as little as three to five weeks. An interesting fact that arises from this method is that although the cuttings have been rooted in water, the roots are not brittle and resemble those on young plants rooted in compost. The reason for this is that after initially filling the container with water, and topping it up again the following morning, it is allowed to evaporate somewhat. This means that at the time of rooting the cuttings are really standing in very moist perlite and not water.

Note: I do not find that I have to keep topping the pot up with water, although I do feel the weight of it from time to time to check that it has not become too dry.

When just nicely rooted, fill a 4" or 5" pot with potting compost and prick out the young plants around the edge of the pot (about a finger width apart – see Multi-Plant Two method on page 38) then place several in the middle. Several weeks later you should be seeing signs of new growth showing in the leaves — *they will brighten in colour.* Once they look to be well established, pinch out the flowering tip of each plant to encourage them to send out fresh shoots. This new growth is going to give you batch after batch of cutting material through the winter, not in March or April from your older rested plants, but perhaps even in November and December. — *grow these* 'mother plants' *on and they themselves can make marvellous plants in the coming season.*

Note: Although individual plants from semi-ripe cuttings do not usually make very good bush plants they will, if you do not remove the growing tip, grow through the flowering stage to make beautiful Standards for the following year.

Authors Note

We have now reached a stage where it could easily become confusing. Here we are at the end of the chapter on propagation and yet there is still another way that I start my plants to describe. There is also a chance, if I am not careful, of traditional methods getting mixed up with my new approach to growing fuchsias — the Multi-Plant method. So, I think it would be best if the next chapter deals with multi-planting, beginning first of all with my latest method of starting them off, then telling you about some of the many aspects of multi-planting that interest me.

Hopefully, my comments will give you an insight into the benefits of multi-planting and also, because topics of this new cultural method are scattered throughout the book it will let you return to one place for the main points should you wish to refer to them again later.

Multi-Planting Fuchsias

I can honestly say that since the idea of growing many plants in a pot, instead of the traditional one, first came into my head in 1991 almost all aspects of my fuchsia culture have changed for the better. The strange thing is that we have been using the techniques I have developed for Multi-Plants on other varieties of plant for years, but never related them to fuchsias. Look around any Garden Centre, for instance, and you will see that many popular house plants are *NOT* grown from a single plant but are made up of several. Can you explain for instance why, when we saw our first 'Pot Mum' Chrysanthemum, which is always developed from five plants placed around the edge of a pot, we didn't think *'That's a good idea'*, I'll grow my fuchsias like that.

I find it even harder to believe that we have always made up hanging pots, baskets and large display plants of fuchsias by placing several established plants together — enjoyed the marvellous results — then, when potting up fuchsias into a plant pot we stick in just one. I can't get over how barmy we have been. I have increasingly become to believe that we have, except for Standards and perhaps the showbench, been growing our fuchsias the wrong way.

It has been such a fascinating period for me as I have developed the Multi-Plant method, learning new techniques as I have gone along and enjoying the benefits of growing fuchsias so easily. In this chapter I will let you know all that I have learnt and also give you my thoughts on how it will improve most, if not all traditional cultural methods.

Note: I have evolved three ways of starting Multi-Plant Fuchsias:
a) Multi-Plant-One is developed from cuttings rooted in a Coffee Jar (see page 37. b) Multi-Plant-Two begins with cuttings being pricked out after being rooted in a propagator (see page 38), and c) Multi-Plant-Three which I will describe below. Reading about method three before methods one and two may seem a little strange, but as it involves an alternative way of taking cuttings I thought it best to place it next to the chapter on propagation.

So, let me begin the cultural side of this chapter by explaining this latest multi-plant development which is simply an extension of *Multi-Plant One*.

I had noticed that plants produced by that method were less prone to losses than those that had had their roots disturbed by being pricked out into a pot. My thoughts led me to thinking of striking, and growing on, cuttings in larger pots than the 2½" pot used in the coffee jar. The only problem, to my mind, was that traditionally we have always used cutting compost to root cuttings, and I certainly did not want to grow on my young plants in a 3½" or larger pot which had little or no nutrients in the compost. The answer I came up with was simple, we do not need to use cutting compost. We can root them in the same compost that we use to grow them on. Just try this method and see how easy it is to grow absolutely marvellous plants. Almost all my plants are now started this way, and this is how it is done:

Multi-Plant-Three: Mix 6 parts of any peat based multi-purpose compost (Levington Potting or similar — *Remember, based on sphagnum or Irish moss peat.*) 1 part of perlite and 1 part of grit or coarse sand and moisten it until you reach the stage when it just does not drip water when squeezed quite hard in your hand. Now, fill a 3½" pot with the moistened compost and firm it slightly to make sure that there are no gaps in the pot, fill it to the top again then pat and smooth the surface to make it level. Prepare about a dozen cuttings, small tip cuttings are best, and as even in size as possible. Then, using a short pointed piece of split cane as a small dibber, place the 8 most even sized cuttings (about a finger width apart) around the edge of the pot (there is no need for rooting powder) and about a third of an inch inboard from the rim so that they do not touch the side. Then put at least one in the middle (a few extra, I use five or six, in the middle will give you some spares in case of losses) and slightly firm all the cuttings in.

All that you now need is a small clear polythene freezer bag (freezer bags tend not to collapse) to place over the pot and an elastic band to hold it in place. Fold the bag lengthwise into two and cut off the corner so that you get a hole your finger can poke through in the centre of the top, this is to allow excess humidity to escape. Then fit the bag on the pot keeping it as tall as possible and place it in a cool, shady place. Dependent on temperature they can root in as little as 4 weeks in summer and 6 or 7 weeks during the winter period. When you see the leaves brightening in colour you can start to harden them off by removing the elastic band to allow air to circulate through the bag, leaving the pot in the same area where they rooted. After a few days, perhaps a week, you should be able to remove the bag altogether (still leave the pot in the same place for a few days more before placing them in your normal growing area) and grow the plants on using the advice on Multi-Plants as described elsewhere in the book.

Some points to note are:

- It is wise to check through the cuttings about twice a week to remove any showing signs of rotting (Botrytis) and replace any lost with some of the spares. I am also quite happy to transplant the little plants around a little if it makes the outer ring of plants more even.

- If you have excessive losses you may well blame me for telling you to moisten the compost so heavily. But it is not that, look at the bag, you will probably find that there is heavy condensation on the inside. Now, what causes condensation? *STEAM!* And what causes steam? *HEAT!* It is not that the compost is too wet, it is too *HOT!* Place the pot in a cooler, shadier position and losses should greatly diminish or cease altogether.

- If you try this method and lose everything, *PLEASE* do not say what a ridiculous way of growing fuchsias and go back to traditional methods. There is *NO* skill in rooting them, all that is required is for you to find a place where they will not get too hot. I root a very high proportion of mine, but let me stress that it is not my skill that is the secret, it is just that I have managed to shade the area where the pots are placed to give me the *RIGHT* conditions.

Note: Let me state again — I no longer use bottom heat to root cuttings. It takes a little longer to root them in the gentle warmth of the greenhouse or home but what is the hurry when we are saving so much time by growing Multi-Plants. You will find that if you root your cuttings in potting compost and in cool conditions they will make much sturdier, healthier plants and because of that, less chance of them being attacked by Botrytis.

You may well, of course, have your own very successful method of rooting cuttings. In which case your can use the **Multi-Plant Two** method and prick them out when rooted as described below.

Pricking Out: Take a suitably sized pot (I almost always use a 3½" pot) and fill it to the top with compost, lightly firm it to make sure there are no air pockets and you are ready to start pricking out. Make a hole of sufficient depth with your index finger and insert a rooted cutting (before the roots get too big), smooth some compost over the roots and very lightly firm it in. Continue planting cuttings, about a finger width apart, until you have circled the pot, then place one or more in the middle. To make it even more interesting try alternating two contrasting coloured cultivars (cuttings must be taken at the same time) around the edge.

How Many Plants to a Pot? This depends entirely on how many rooted cuttings are available. If, for instance, you have only five I would place them into a 2½" pot; six or seven would go into a 3" pot; eight or nine into a 3½" pot, etc. The rule I apply is that the plants around the edge of the pot should be spaced out approximately a finger width (I use the narrow part of my index finger — a lady or anyone with small hands should perhaps use the wider part) apart. An important point with multi-planting is that you should *ALWAYS* have at least one plant in the middle, this is to fill in the hole that occurs after the outer plants have been leant outwards. My reasoning for having plants so close together is that they naturally grow into a nice symmetrical shape, on the other hand plants placed half a mile (a slight exaggeration) apart need training to make branches cover the bare areas.

Note: The above is how I approach growing fuchsias by the multi-plant method. You, of course, may amend them to use whatever number of plants you are comfortable with. It may even be that you will evolve a system in which you use a different number of plants dependent on which cultivar you are using, e.g. fewer plants for bushy types and more for long jointed ones — just tailor my ideas to suit your needs.

Watering: Great care must be taken when watering Multi-Plants during the early stages (all small plants in comparatively large pots for that matter), because if they are overwatered they will almost certainly succumb to Botrytis or Root Rot. The easy way of explaining how to water them is to compare it to watering summer bedding plants after planting them out in the garden — with these plants we normally give them a good soaking. Now, if they stayed as wet as we leave them they also would rot off, but they don't do they, the water seeps away into the surrounding soil to leave the plants in moist ground. We can use the same principle of watering that we use successfully in the garden with young plants growing in pots. Simply moisten the surface (I always water from the top) of the compost with a washing-up liquid container or anything else that will dribble water gently into the pot, until you gauge the compost is wet to the depth of the roots. Excess water should now percolate into the drier compost towards the bottom of the pot, continue to water in this manner until the plants are well established and growing on healthily.

Note: Do not water Multi-Plants until the compost starts to show signs that it is beginning to dry out — composts based on Sphagnum or Irish moss peat fade in colour as they dry out. Only then start to give some water using the above method. The water I use always contains 10mm (2 teaspoons) of 'Maxicrop Original' to the gallon.

Pinching Out: The amount of pinching out you do is entirely up to you. You can have beautiful large plants without any pinching out at all if you use plenty of cuttings — the Non Stop Fuchsia is with us at last. Dependent on the number of plants used you can give them just one or two stops and you are growing plants of almost show quality. As a guideline let me tell you how and when I decide to give my Multi-Plants their first pinch. First of all it depends on the cultivar that I am dealing with. Some are fairly short jointed and can be allowed to grow 4 or 5 sets of leaves before pinching out, cultivars with medium gaps between the leaves are stopped at around three sets. Those with longer joints, however, are better pinched at 2 sets to get as many shoots as possible at the base of the plant. My subsequent pinches are done at one or two sets of leaves, again dependent on how long the joints are between leaves, and always to keep the symmetrical shape of the plant.

Dependant on when you take your cuttings you can do the following: **a)** September through to March — give the young plants several pinches out, we do not need to have flowering plants too early in the season. **b)** March and April — give them one stop. May and June — grow a non stop fuchsia. **c)** As an ex-exhibitor I still build up my plants by pinching out until I get a fairly *busy* head (plenty of shoots), once that stage is reached growth is allowed to continue until I see buds appearing in the growing tips. If by that time the growth is sturdy enough to support the weight of flowers, it is allowed to flower. On the other hand, if growth is getting a bit *leggy* I give the plant a final pinch, taking it back to perhaps one set of leaves above it's last pinch, but always to keep the lovely round shape. By this time the plant will possibly have had three or four pinches out, and because it was in bud when I last pinched it out it will produce buds again almost immediately, thus helping to keep the plant in shape when in full flower. Timing the plants for a show or a particular time is much easier because they flower in show condition for a much longer period than the traditional *'one in a pot'* plant — this is because they are much younger, have had little or no root disturbance, and have been kept growing on. I just try and make sure that I give the plant sufficient time after it's last pinch to ensure it is in full flower before the required date.

Note: With long jointed cultivars like Triphyllas or 'Checkerboard' I would recommend the use of more plants in the pot, and also making the initial pinch quite low down to encourage as many shoots from the base of the plants as possible. This, and pinching out at each pair of leaves, will then make it much easier to get the essential 'busy' head.

Training: The laborious training of Bushes, Baskets and Hanging Pots has gone. Multi-Plants are almost self shaping. Because the cuttings are very soft and of the same size they invariably root at almost the same time, consequently they tend to grow at the same rate. My simple training is as follows: When the plants are about a couple of inches high I simply stroke the outer ones away from the centre to splay them out a bit, and I will do this several times until I give the plant (please start to think of it as one plant) it's first pinch out. If you look at it before pinching you should see that the symmetrical shape you have been dreaming about is almost in-built, all that you have to do is take out the growing tip of each of the young plants.

Note: If you find that the odd plant or shoot is a little behind, do not pinch it out at the same time as the others. Let it catch up, then pinch it out to the shape of the plant. Do this whenever you are shaping your plants.

The next stage of training starts when the stems of the young plants start firm up a little. I then place my finger at the base of each of the outer ones and tilt them over towards the wall of the pot so that they start to take on a more horizontal position. This splaying out of the plants can be repeated each time I pot up the plant — *see note on next page*. One other thing to note is that, because the pot the plants were rooted in was filled to the top with compost, it will now be necessary to make sure that after potting up that there is sufficient space above the top of the compost for watering, this often entails teasing out some of compost off the bottom of the rootball —*always ensure when potting up that there is ample space at the top of the pot for watering. Remember that when plants are potbound roots can start to push the compost upwards and take away some of the watering space.* The only other training that I do is to carefully bring out sideways any lower sideshoots of the outer ring of plants, and give the plant an occasional stroke to bring the growth downwards. When you look at it, all the training of these plants involves is: Pinch out to the shape of the head, some leaning out when potting up, and quite a lot stroking. You really have to try it to believe it!

Note: There is no single set of rules for the tilting or leaning out of the outer plants when potting up. You will probably find, as I do, that the amount of tilting depends on the type of cultivar that you are growing. For instance, some cultivars have very stiff, upright growing, woody branches and these would benefit from being leant out several times to avoid them showing bare lower stems as they get older. Others have branches in which the wood is much weaker and in fact bends under the weight of the flowers. This type of cultivar does not need to be leaned out quite as much, and would also be better with some sort of support, e.g. split canes, given to the plants. The amount of tilting also depends on whether you are going to grow your Multi-Plants into bush shapes or are developing them for basket growth.

Multi-Varieties: One of the exciting cultural bonuses that has emerged from multi-planting is that two or more different cultivars can now be grown in the same pot or container, you can even mix singles and doubles. In every instance I have found not only have the different cultivars grown together to become one plant, but also that the flowers start to develop at the same time. And even if one is slightly before the other, because Multi-Plants flower for such a long period, you will have the whole plant in flower for a considerable time.

My advice should you wish to grow more than one type of cultivar in a pot is to take the tip cuttings at the same time but root them in a propagator or separate pots first. Then, when rooted and hardened off, but well before the roots get too vigorous, prick them out into a pot. I normally start them off in a 4¼" half pot, placing 10 plants of one cultivar around the edge (a finger width apart) and about 5 cuttings of another contrasting coloured cultivar in the middle. As they grow you may have to do a little pruning of the inner or outer shoots as you don't want the different cultivars bleeding into each other. Another formation that I have found pleasing is to alternate two different cultivars as you prick them out. Try these methods, they work and are very interesting.

Note: I think that you will get the best out of multi-cultivar Multi-Plants by growing them on into a second year and into larger pots.

Feeding & Growing on: These are other aspects of culture where I have slightly amended my usual methods to better suit the growing of Multi-Plants. Young plants in their earliest stages *MUST NOT* be liquid fed, however, I do use seaweed extract *'Maxicrop Original'* (not a feed but a plant growth stimulant) from the beginning, using it at a weak (10mm per gallon) strength. Feeding starts when the plants have developed three or four sets of leaves and the stems and roots are starting to get stronger. The feed I use for this early stage of growth is Fisons Liquinure used at a quarter strength (10mm per gallon) and in conjunction with the seaweed extract. As Multi-Plants are kept growing on and do not have a traditional dormant season I feed my plants throughout winter. Remember, I do grow my plants in a slightly heated greenhouse — but even if I did not I would give them a feed whenever I had need to water them, which in a cool place wouldn't be that often.

I do believe that we have to forget tradition, and perhaps do things that have never been recommended before if we are going to get the best out of this new approach to growing fuchsias. As I have just mentioned I keep my Multi-Plants growing on, so if a plant needs potting on in October it is potted on and if the same plant fills its pot with roots again by December or January, it is potted on again. It is because the plants are kept ticking over (even if you are going to keep them in cooler situations than I do through winter, I would still follow the above advice) that they develop into such lovely plants so quickly. By treating them this way they are kept in green leaf to give you a winter full of interest — you will also find that cutting material is available much earlier, another plus for this idea.

Vine Weevil: Although it is early days yet with this new way of growing, one of the by-products of the Multi-Plant method is that for several winters now I have not been troubled with the dreaded Vine Weevil, losing only the odd plant, far less than I have ever lost in the past with the traditional methods of cultivation. Although, when you think about it is perhaps not too surprising. Vine Weevil grubs feed on the thick tap roots or the crowns of older plants and do not seem to bother young plants too much. So it would be a not too bright adult Vine Weevil that laid eggs in a pot full of young plants where there is no food supply for it's young. Perhaps the greatest plus with Multi-Plants is that you grow big young plants *NOT* big old plants.

Confidence: Once you have the confidence that Multi-Plants started in the spring of one year will become quite large flowering plants by the summer of the next you will find, as I do, that there is no need to keep big old plants through another winter. In fact, the only plants that I take through a second winter are just a few for baskets or patio tubs. You also need confidence to grow, and flower, many plants in a 3½" pot. You will find that there is no need, especially if the cultivar is a small flowered one, to keep potting up. Just treat Multi-Plants as you would one plant in a pot.

Pot Size: I have found that my best Multi-Plants are started off in quite small pots, mainly the 3½" size. The reason of this is that you get several chances to lean the plants outwards as you pot them up. If you start them off in large pots you can usually only lean them out once — the result of leaning out plants is that you no longer see those unsightly bare stems at the base of your fuchsias.

Multi-Plant versus Single Plant: It is very interesting to make up a multi-plant and a single plant from the same batch of cuttings, grow them on and compare the quality of growth at a later date. You will probably find, as I do, that the single plant makes the poorer one. Here are some of the differences I have noticed: **a)** Foliage on plants in a Multi-Plant cover the surface of the compost very quickly, whereas on the single plant the compost is open to the sun for a very long time. **b)** A canopy of growth soon develops on the Multi-Plant to shade the pot, thus maintaining the compost at a more even temperature and moisture content. **c)** In the same period of time the single plant makes as much root as the multi-plant. **d)** Roots on the single plant wrap round and round the pot, on multi-plants they don't. **e)** In the initial stages of growth leaves grow larger on the single plant than on the multi-plant. **f)** Certain cultivars just will not grow evenly as a single plant. So, as a grower I find it hard to get my head around the fact that when I multi-plant these awkward, but often beautiful fuchsias, they tend to grow as round as a bobbin.

Note: I honestly believe that the single plant in a pot behaves as it does because it feels threatened. Try and imagine what a plant feels like when the compost becomes overheated every time the sun shines. I am convinced that the plant makes extra root, grows larger leaves and sends shoots out in all directions to compensate for the awful environment in which it is living. To prove to yourself whether I am right or not try multi-planting all those cultivars that you stopped growing because they would not grow evenly and enjoy the lovely symmetrical plants that you produce.

Roots Growing Through the Bottom of the Pot: Whilst giving a cultural demonstration at the Malvern Autumn Show a lady pointed out to me that the roots of my plants weren't growing through the bottom of the pot. This query led me to wonder WHY there was no sign of roots, when roots always did escape from my pots with traditional cultural methods. The answer that I came up with was that plants do not do this if they are getting all the nutrients they need from the compost within the pot. It is only when the requirements of the plant are not met that the roots go in search of essential nutrients elsewhere.

This then led me to ask myself another question. Why don't roots on Multi-Plants leave the pot, even when they have been in the same pot for quite a long period? The answer, I believe, lies in the fact that one of the great benefits of growing fuchsias by the Multi-Plant method is that by using many plants in a pot the resultant flowering plant is still quite young. Consequently the pot is full of fibrous roots that all help to feed the plant. On the other hand, however, a plant of similar size grown by traditional methods could be several years old with a considerable amount of quite large tap roots. These big thick roots, which in nature are developed to secure the plant in the ground, are useless to a plant growing in a pot, they just take up valuable room and limit the amount of fibrous feeder roots available to the plant. If the plant cannot take up sufficient nutrients for its needs from within the pot then roots obviously will need to go in search for more.

Tap Roots: It seems strange now, looking back at how I traditionally grew my plants, that I didn't think of the problems that arise when keeping plants for many years in a pot. I can remember potting plants down in spring, removing old compost and trying to get the rootball into a smaller pot as advised, only to find that I had to poke a small amount of compost between the roots with a piece a split cane and frequently tap the pot on the bench. I know that I would probably pot them up a little later in the

31

season, but this extra compost still did not give sufficient fibrous root area to supply quite large plants with all the nutrients they required when in full flower. Hence, in my opinion, the reason for bud drop in the heat of summer and the tendency of plants to flush flower. On the other hand the equivalent sized Multi-Plant seem to never want to stop flowering, with sets of tiny new buds following on one after other. The reason for the change is, I believe, the fact that pots with Multi-Plants in them are full of fibrous feeder roots and not three quarters full of, useless to the plant, big thick tap roots.

How Long do you Keep Them? You can obviously keep them for as long as you wish, but I think you will be back to square one if they are kept so long that the plants fill the pot with big, old tap roots. The system that I have evolved sees me starting off multi-plants throughout the year, those started during the early months are allowed to flower during the season —are potted up in late autumn — and kept growing on through winter to become much larger plants the following summer. These plants will not be taken on through another winter unless I want a few for baskets or patio tubs. Plants started later in the summer are again kept growing on through the winter, giving you batch after batch of cuttings, to give you glorious 5" or 6" pot plants the following year. The oldest plants that I now have will have only seen two winters and three summers at most.

When you think about it, perhaps the greatest pleasures we have with fuchsias is propagation and the developing of plants. Keeping them for ever and a day takes a great deal of that pleasure away.

Getting Older? Do not think, because of impaired sight or infirmity that you cannot enjoy the pleasures of Multi-Plants. Just because I recommend the use of tiny tip cuttings it doesn't mean that it can't be done any other way. Take cuttings any way that you can comfortably manage, but take them in good numbers so that you can prick them out as described earlier. The very fact that you are growing several plants in a pot will make a considerable improvement to the results that you used to get with one.

Conclusion: I have been growing Multi-Plants for several years now and realise that this is how we should always have been growing fuchsias. The quality of plants has to be seen to be believed, it is as though you have lifted the vigour and flowering capacity of a garden fuchsia and placed it into a pot. It really is Mind-Boggling!

Growing a Bush or Shrub Fuchsia

What is the difference between a Bush and Shrub Fuchsia? The British Fuchsia Society Judges and Exhibitors Handbook says that a bush must be developed on a single stem not exceeding 1½", and that a shrub has more than one shoot emerging from below ground level. The following statement applies to both forms of growth: *'The entire plant should be covered with an abundance of foliage and flower, presenting a balanced symmetrical plant when viewed from all angles'*. In this chapter I will describe how I grow fuchsias to the above description from a single plant, and also a much easier way of producing the same effect from my own cultural development — the *Multi-Plant*. Both methods will be of help, especially to the beginner, in the aim to grow better shaped plants that are more pleasing to the eye and that produce more flowers.

SINGLE PLANT

Bi-annual Method: Cuttings are usually taken during May or June and plants continually developed by pinching out the growing tips (after the initial pinch at 3 or 4 sets of leaves) at each pair of leaves whenever growth allows. Plants are usually not allowed to flower in their first season and are best limited to 3½" half pots until autumn when they should be potted on into 3½" full pots and overwintered in frost free conditions, or better still grown on in gentle warmth. When spring comes around they should be potted on into 4", then 5" or 6" pots to make marvellous flowering plants for the summer.

Overview of my Method: I have successfully grown Show Plants from cuttings taken in all months of the year, but find that the best time for propagation is during the period September to March when growth is much more short jointed. Young plants are grown on to the following description and pot size limited to 4" for plants started in the later months of the year and 3½" for those taken after the shortest day (I do not use 5" pots until plants are at least 12 months old). I find that not overpotting in the first year helps to build up a firm framework of growth which is of great benefit when growing plants on into larger pots in the future years of their life.

Plants started from cuttings taken during late spring and summer are trained by pinching out growth until they come into bud, then allowed to flower even if they are only in 3" pots. My thoughts are that if a plant wants to flower let it flower, enjoy their beauty for the summer, then lightly prune them back and start to grow them on again in the autumn.

MY METHOD

I start by placing my rooted cutting centrally in a small pot, usually the 2" size, but for the occasional vigorous rooted cultivar it could be a 2½" pot. I do this for two reasons:

- It is not good practice to place any plant with a small root system into a large amount of compost, especially in the cool growing conditions that most of us have to contend with in the early part of the year.

- My main objective is to keep the growth of my bush plants compact. I find that starting young plants off in small pots produces shorter stems between leaves.

The young plant will now start to grow and should be turned by a third every few days to ensure even growth. After a period of three or four weeks be on the lookout for roots starting to show through the drainage holes at the base of the pot. This, and the top growth which should now be filling out above the pot, tell me that it is time to check if the plant needs potting on.

Remove the plant from its pot and examine the root system. I like to see roots showing in all parts of the compost before I pot on, but be careful not to allow the plant to become potbound (roots going round and round). Once the potting on stage is reached I move the plant into a slightly larger pot. My potting up stages are from 2" to 2½" – 2½" to 3" – 3" to 3½" – 3½" to 4" – 4" to 5" and 5" to 6". Again, this is done for the reason mentioned above, to help keep growth compact.

One tip on potting up is to use the *FORMER* method. This is where you take a clean pot, the size into which you wish to place the plant, and put a small amount of slightly moist compost in the bottom. Now take an empty pot, the same size as the one in which the plant has bccn growing, and place it inside the larger one with the tops level. Pour compost over them both and with a short piece of cane of suitably diameter, poke it down between the pots until you fill the gap. Gently take out the inner pot, remove the plant from its own pot and place it in the form that you have just made. Lightly firm it in (perlite and grit in the compost allow this) and you have potted up your plant without it knowing it has been moved and, more importantly, without damage.

While the plant has been developing its root system the top will have been growing. When you can see three sets of sideshoots on the main stem, carefully remove the growing tip — *this is called stopping or pinching out*. Six sideshoots are my ideal number to use when growing a bush. The four lower ones face outwards in a north, south, east and west configuration, the upper pair help to fill in the top. You can now allow the plant to grow on until it is ready for its second stop. This takes place after the bottom sideshoots have developed enough growth to stop them at three sets of leaves, the middle ones at two sets of leaves, and the top ones, no matter how long they have grown, at one set of leaves. On some long jointed cultivars, this stop may have to be at two sets of leaves on the bottom pair, two on the middle and one at the top.

This SHAPING stop should have given the young plant width at the base, and kept the height down. It should already be taking on a roundish or mushroom shape. Allow the new sideshoots from the six branches to grow until they have one set of leaves, or two if it is a short jointed cultivar, then pinch out all the growing points again, making sure that you don't miss any — *having said that, it is not unusual for me to allow any retarded shoots to continue with their growth until they reach the outer edge of the plant and then pinch them out*. Continue stopping the shoots at every pair or two pairs of leaves and always for shape, gradually building up the plant until the end of May, or the middle of June at the latest. Remember, every time you stop a plant you delay flowering by a minimum of eight weeks. So if you continue pinching out into July or August the season could be over before you see any flowers. Allowing a plant to grow on from its last stop in May or early June, should give you a beautiful show of flowers from at least August onwards.

No one can tell you exactly how long a plant will take to flower after its last stop. It can depend on so many things, i.e. type of cultivar, weather, daylight length, etc. However, if you wish to time your plant for a show, or a particular date, I would suggest that you allow approximately ten weeks for a single or semi-double flowered cultivar and twelve weeks or more for a double. Reduce these times by at least two weeks if flower buds are showing in the tips of the shoots. Always make a note of the date of your last stop, and also when the plant is in full flower until you become familiar with the stopping times for your particular cultivars. This information will help you to adjust your timing in future years.

Here is a list of points that I think are important:

- Place rooted cuttings into small pots and pot up in half inch stages up to the 4" size.

- Pot up when the roots have moved into all parts of the compost, not when they are only just showing or the plant has become potbound.

- Do not be over ambitious in pot size when growing a bush fuchsia in its first few months of life. I also think it is a mistake to place any plant other than a vigorous growing cultivar in anything over a 5" pot in its first year (my own plants are limited to 3½" or 4" pots).

- Remember, a great many cultivars have small to medium sized flowers. These make beautiful flowering plants if kept in 3½" or 4" pots for their first season.

- Stop your plants as soon as the growing points can be safely removed without damaging the emerging sideshoots, not when you have to remove several pairs of leaves. Letting sideshoots grow too long simply wastes the plant's energy, and new growth will not emerge as readily from the already hardening wood.

- The penultimate stop is just as important as the last. Make sure that you have enough growth for the last stop by leaving four or five weeks between the two pinches.

- You should be looking for flower buds approximately five weeks before the show as it is amazing how long it takes a bud to open from when it is first noticed. You can regulate the time a plant comes into flower a little by placing it in cooler conditions (greenhouse floor) if it is too advanced, or in a warmer, sunnier position if it is late.

Training your Bush Fuchsia: I start to train the growth of my plants from the time that they are in 3" pots. My aim is to position the *SOFT* branches so that they are equally spaced around the edge of the pot, and also to bend them down to just above the horizontal. For most of this work

I use short pieces of plastic coated garden wire bent over into 'WALKING STICK' shapes. I insert these into the slightly firmed compost to pull the branches down. It is amazing how much you can improve a plant by placing branches where YOU want them to grow, rather than allowing the plant to grow as nature intended.

Two points to note are:

* Do NOT try to bend branches in which the wood has hardened.
* Do NOT firm your compost unless you have included perlite and grit.

MULTI-PLANT METHOD

This new growing technique of mine which started, in some ways, by accident has turned out to be a completely new approach to the cultivation of fuchsias, in fact it could almost be called a breakthrough. My latest development of the method, 'Multi-Plant-Three' is described at the beginning of the last chapter but as Multi-Plants can be started in various ways let me now explain Methods One and Two:

Note: You will have to excuse the fact that Multi-Plant-Three comes before methods one and two but as it included a different way of taking cuttings I thought it best to place it next to the chapter on propagation — just put it down to my eccentric way of writing.

Multi-Plant-One: This method starts with something that we discussed earlier, the coffee jar propagator — see page 14. Prepare 8 tip cuttings of even size and of the same cultivar. Insert the cuttings (7 around the edge and 1 in the middle) of a 2½" plastic pot and root them, using a multi-purpose soilless potting compost in place of the sphagnum moss peat in the cutting compost (you can also root them straight into potting compost as we did in the Multi-Plant-Three method if you wish) harden them off, and we are ready for the next stage.

The above method of propagation can only be thought unusual because of the small size of the cutting material. Cuttings have always been placed around the edge of a pot to root. The amazing thing is that once rooted everyone would then individually pot up the young plants to grow them on for a period, before possibly bringing them all back together in a hanging pot or basket. Ridiculous isn't it! Lets try a more sensible method. Instead of potting up the young plants individually as is the normal practice, wait until they have developed enough roots to hold the compost together, then pot them up as one unit, into a 3" pot. From now on you are going to treat the plants as one plant. Just think about the benefits of this! If you pinch out the growing tip of a single young plant at three sets of leaves you get 6 sideshoots. But if you pinch out the growing tips of our young plant, made up of eight plants, at three sets of leaves you can have as many as 48 sideshoots (try stopping at 4 or 5 sets of leaves for even more sideshoots). On some cultivars you do not even need another stop, although I would advise you to give one (if time permits) as a second stop at two sets of leaves on each of the 48 sideshoots would give you nearly 200 new shoots. The results of growing a bush by using this method are almost mind-boggling! Other advantages of this method are:

- Shaping and Training the plant are easily done as described on page 27 in the last chapter.

- Perhaps the greatest gain will be with the large flowering doubles. The only fault, if you can call it a fault, with this type of plant is that they usually do not carry too many flowers, just try growing a cultivar like 'Swingtime' with this method and see what happens.

- You may think, because the multi-plant has been developed so quickly, that the growth would not support the weight of the flowers, but you would be wrong. Somehow the stems and shoots seem to have much more substance about them than those on the traditional, much older, fuchsia grown from a single plant. As a fuchsia grower, you will get a great many cultural surprises as you get used to this new approach to their culture. Time and again you will be proved wrong when you try things that your mind tells you won't work.

Multi-Plant-Two: This method differs from the above only in that you start the cuttings off in an 8½" by 6" propagator or whichever way you use for propagation. Take tip cuttings in numbers of at least 5 but preferably 8 or 10. When rooted, harden them off from the high humidity of the propagator, then prick out (see page 24) 7 around the edge and one in the middle of a 3½" pot and grow them on as described in the last chapter.

Several points that I would like you to be aware of when growing Multi-Plants are:

- Growing a bush plant by this method works best if you use the soft growing tips of shoots for your cuttings. The reason for this is that tip cuttings root almost at the same time (long cuttings don't) and after potting up grow at the same rate. Because of this the multiple plants virtually become one plant, so much so that when the plant is in flower it is impossible to distinguish it from one grown from a single cutting.

- Although it is traditionally advisable to grow only one type of cultivar in a pot or basket, it will be of interest to try more than one because with the plants being raised from tip cuttings of the same age the different cultivars, even singles and doubles, tend to match each other for growth and flower at similar times.

- If you use the Multi-Plant-Two method prick out the young plants whilst the roots are at an early stage of development, otherwise you will have an almost impossible task to achieve.

- Take great care when watering in the early stages (see page 25), it is easy to lose a plant because of over-watering. An ideal aid to watering small pots or plants is a washing-up liquid container.

- Because the plant is made up of several plants it will need potting on sooner than a single plant, but do not pot up into a larger pot than you would normally use, there is no need. My potting on stages for Multi-Plants are 3½" – 4¼", 4¼" – 5", 5" – 6" (the extra width of the 4¼" pot, as opposed to a 4" pot, allows that touch more space for the plants to be leant outwards.

Note: I am now finding that I do not have to pot on, as is traditionally done, whenever roots start to fill the pot. Somehow the roots on multi-plants are entirely different to those produced by the single plant and perhaps are better not potted up quite as freely. Try keeping multi-plants in smaller pots yourself to get a feeling of the difference.

- Do not liquid feed Multi-Plants any differently than you would a single plant, just be aware that they will need feeding a week or two sooner (more information on feeding in chapters 4 & 13).

- Do not allow foliage in the centre of the plant to become too dense, remove some of the larger leaves to let air circulate, also be constantly on the lookout for, and remove, damaged leaves inside the plant.

Do not hesitate to try multi-planting, it works. Play about with the different methods I have described and tailor them to your own requirements. I can only emphasise that this new approach to growing has improved almost every aspect of my fuchsia culture.

Growing a Basket

Firstly I will explain how I grow a Full Basket to exhibition quality in the traditional way — growing plants on individual, then planting them up into the basket in spring. Many, if not all, of the points that I make will apply to all types of hanging container, so it should only be a matter of adapting them to suit the one that you wish to use. Later in the chapter I will tell you about a much easier and, I believe, a better way of growing a basket, under the heading 'Baskets the Easy Way'.

TRADITIONAL METHOD

If you intend exhibiting your baskets please refer to the show schedule as to the type of basket allowed for that particular show. Some societies state that baskets must be hemispherical whilst others allow them to have a flat bottom. There is nothing more frustrating than, having perhaps grown the best basket of your life, finding that the container you have grown it in does not conform to the rules.

There are two comments I would like to make at this stage:

• Although there is no rule to prevent you from using more than one type of cultivar in your basket or hanging pot, I personally believe that if you plant them up using traditional methods you will have far better results if they are the same. My reason for saying this is that plants in a basket of mixed fuchsias, having been grown for some considerable time in individual pots, will have different growth habits and flowering times.

  Note: See Chapter 4 on 'Multi-Planting' fuchsias for my latest thoughts on this topic.

• Do put enough plants in your container, it will then fill and cascade over the edge more quickly. I would suggest for a:

14" Full Basket: Six plants from 3½" pots, five round the edge and one in the middle.

12" Full Basket: Five plants from 3½" pots, Four round the edge and one in the middle.

14" Half Basket: Five plants from 3½" pots, three round the front and two across the back.

8" Hanging Pot: Five plants from 2½" pots, four round the edge and one in the middle.

6" Hanging Pot: Three plants from 2½" pots equally spaced round the edge.

Notes: a) Do not be afraid of using more than the number of plants stated if your chosen cultivar has weak growth or the plants are not very large. b) To have plants in 3½" pots ready for planting up in spring cuttings need to be taken around August and grown on through winter, 2½" pots are best started in December or January. c) An improvement to the traditional planting up of baskets is to use more than one plant in each pot, e.g. the Multi-Plant method.

The first decision to make when growing a fuchsia basket is which cultivar to use. Of course, you only need to go to any garden centre or nursery in spring to see fuchsias recommended for basket work, but to my mind the growth on many of them is far too weak. Consequently it cannot support any weight and usually results in a basket having a bare top with a fringe of flowers around the lower edge of the trailing shoots. In my opinion a basket is a poor one if it does not have a crown that is at least as high as the depth of the container.

I usually start looking for cultivars to use in my baskets during the previous season. I look for plants that cover themselves with flowers, have branches that have enough strength to support the flowers, yet are supple enough to trail with the extension of growth that you usually get when growing fuchsias in hanging containers. Having made your decision, either obtain enough young plants for your needs, or as I do raise your own.

Choose your cuttings carefully, taking them from strong growing shoots. When rooted the young plants are potted into 2" or 2½" pots and kept together, so that whether they are potted on or stopped they are all done at the same time. This is important, for when the basket is made up the plants should be all at the same stage of growth. I like to grow my plants on in pots until they are in the largest size that will comfortably go in the basket — in the case of the 14" size this is a 3½" pot. Once again I think this is an important point. Because the plants are going to be placed in a relatively large amount of compost it is far better that their root systems are as well formed as possible.

I grow the plants on slowly, stopping the growing shoots several times to create a bushy habit, at a temperature of around 45° Fahrenheit until about mid March when, with luck, they are well rooted and ready to be planted up. If they are not quite ready I wait a few weeks longer until the plants are well rooted. The compost I use is a peat based multi-purpose potting one with my usual perlite and grit added to aid drainage. The plastic coated wire baskets that I use are lined with black polythene that is liberally pierced around the base to allow excess water to escape. I place the lined basket on a large bucket to hold it firm and half fill it with compost, then taking the six most evenly balanced plants I remove their lower leaves so that they will not be lying on the compost. I do this to help prevent plants being attacked by Botrytis (Grey Mould) which can be a bit of a problem when growing baskets.

The next step is to remove the plants from their pots. I then place the tallest plant in the centre of the basket with the other five, leaning slightly outwards, equally spaced around the edge. More compost is now added, gradually filling in and around the plants, finishing with the surface of the compost a good inch below the top of the basket to allow for watering. I now firm (the perlite and grit allow me to do this) the plants in before watering them in with a rose on the can. Wait for the compost to nearly dry out before watering again, and do be careful, this is a critical time for your basket because it is so easy to spoil everything by losing a plant because of overwatering.

The objective when growing a basket is to hide the container with a profusion of foliage and flowers. To help achieve that aim I train the plants so that the young branches are equally spaced over the whole area of the basket, with the lower ones held down towards the horizontal. A useful aid for training this early growth will be pieces of plastic coated garden wire, cut into three or four inch lengths and bent over at one end. These hooks, when pushed into the compost, can be used to train any type of soft growth. Another method that you can use to train growth is to weigh branches down by clipping clothes pegs around the stems at the outer end of the shoots. But do take care not to bend the branches too sharply or to use too much weight. This training and shaping continues until the basket takes on the form of one large plant.

My stopping procedure for baskets is as follows. Allow the shoots on each plant to grow (dependent on how long jointed the growth on the cultivar you use) four, five or even six sets of leaves before pinching out the growing tips, and thereafter at every second pair, treating it as one plant and stopping for shape. Remember, it will take approximately ten weeks for a single or semi-double flowered cultivar, and twelve weeks or more for a double before the basket is in full flower after its last stop. Do make allowances for this if you wish to have a long flowering season, or if you want to exhibit your basket.

To keep the basket in good health and encourage a long flowering season it is advisable to feed regularly with an High Nitrogen or at most a Balanced Feed during the summer months. I would keep off High Potash feeds (unless the basket is in a very shady position) because the last thing you want is for the growth to become so hard that it doesn't trail.

Be careful: Some cultivars grow an abundance of leaves, so much so that they become a solid ball of foliage. With these I remove some of the larger leaves in the middle of the basket to allow air to circulate through the plants. This is done to help prevent that dreaded disease, Botrytis.

Beware: Most manufactured plastic baskets and hanging pots have a saucer attached — *this can be a death trap for fuchsias*. In summer it is so easy to water baskets without checking to see if they need it or not. The saucer then acts as a reservoir, causing the compost to stay permanently wet. The roots, and ultimately the plants, could then die. The simple answer to the problem is to remove the saucer and allow excess water to drain away.

BASKETS THE EASY WAY

I have been developing the Multi-Plant method for some years now and have come to realise that this simple idea really is a breakthrough in fuchsia culture. For far too long we have done things the *traditional* way, purely because that's how it has always been done. Well, let's break with tradition and look at an alternative and much easier method.

This way of growing a basket or hanging pot of fuchsias is a continuation of the 'Multi-Plant' method. One of the advantages gained in growing many fuchsias in a pot is that the growth of the plant (because of stroking down of foliage, leaning out of plants and teasing out of sideshoots see chapters 4 and 5) naturally lends it self to basket use. After trying this way of growing a basket or hanging pot I don't think anyone will revert to growing them by traditional methods.

Notes: a) A point of interest for exhibitors is that these marvellous plants CAN be shown once they are in a basket or hanging pot as the rule for that type of growth is that one or more plants may be used. b) Because of this change in culture it is possible or even recommended to use cultivars with much stiffer growth for your baskets or hanging pots as the leaning outwards of the outer plants means that growth naturally grows sideways. c) If you find that traditional basket cultivars tend to collapse under the weight of flower when using the Multi-Plant method try keeping them in a 5" maximum sized pot for their first season so as to build up a firm framework of branches. This should then help to support growth when grown on and potted up into a basket the following season.

I think the best way for me to explain how to go about developing a basket by this method is to divide growers into two sections, those that have a heated greenhouse to keep their plants gently growing on through winter, and those who haven't:

With a Heated Greenhouse: Having a heated greenhouse really does give you an advantage and opens up other ways of achieving the same quite startling results, but before I describe them let me pass on a tip that has been a boon to me as it has given me much more growing space and made far more use of heat. My advice is to fasten wooden dowelling of a suitable diameter along each side of the roof slope, sufficiently high so that hanging pots suspended from it are well clear of plants on the bench below. Now I'll take you stage by stage through the different methods I use:

Method One: Plants grown from the 'Multi-Plant' method in spring are limited to, and flowered, in 4¼" or 5" half pots during the summer months. Later in the season after they are past their best, perhaps sometime in September or October, lightly cut back the growth to leave a very good overhang (at least the width of your hand) over the edge of the pot. Now pot them up into 6" hanging pots (leaning out the outer plants again as you do so) and hang them up on the dowelling. Even if you only have gentle warmth in winter, the temperature in the roof area will be much higher than at bench level whilst the heater is running, so the plants should soon be showing signs of growth. Pinch out the growing tips of the plant as growth develops during the winter months, shaping it as you do so — *and don't forget to start more Multi-Plants with this wonderful cutting material.* You should also tease out any new shoots growing upwards from around the edge of the plant, and bring them out sideways below the other growth. Basically this, and the occasional stroking down of the foliage is the only training you need do. By February or March, or whenever the plant fills its pot with roots, move the plant on into an 8" hanging pot and allow it to grow on, stopping it again when growth allows. Dependent on the cultivar and the amount of growth that you get you may well be able to pot it on again into a 10" hanging pot or even a full basket.

Further points are:

- Sun can become quite strong through glass in late February or early March so you may have to shade the plants or remove them from the roof area.

- There is no need to continue to grow them on in hanging containers, they can of course be potted on from the hanging pots into larger plant pots or patio tubs.

- Although you can stop pinching out the plant whenever you want and allow it to flower, if you continue to develop it and make your last stop and potting on in early May, you could have a flowering basket or tub of almost mind-boggling proportions sometime in July or August.

Method Two: This method is equally startling but because it starts in early spring is perhaps better suited for smaller hanging containers. All that is needed to start with is plenty of cutting material. Here are my step be step stages of producing a very quick and easy hanging pot:

- Take tip cuttings of your chosen cultivar as early as possible and in quantities of at least ten.

- When rooted, and before the roots become too large, prick out 7 or 8 around the edge of a 3½" pot and place one or more in the middle. You can also, of course, use the Multi-Plant-Three method where cuttings are rooted directly into the pot.

- Now, using the advice in chapter 4, develop the pot of fuchsias until it is ready for potting on, except that growth on each plant should be allowed to produce four or five pairs of leaves. The idea is to get as many shoots as possible coming from the base, then remove all the growing tips.

- When the plant is nicely rooted pot it straight up into a 6" hanging pot and pinch out the growing tips of all the new shoots after one or two pairs leaves have developed — training should be as in Method One.

- Dependent on how early you started you could pot up again into an 8" hanging pot and stop the plant again, but do this by early May.

- Do not hesitate to use a larger number of plants (finger width apart over the whole area of the compost) in perhaps a 4" pot or even straight into a 6" hanging pot if you cannot take your cuttings until later in the season or if the cultivar is not a vigorous growing one. Dependent on how many plants you use you could even get away with only one stop. Try not pinching out at all if you are using a self breaking cultivar.

- Do overwinter your hanging pots, they make superb full baskets or patio tubs the following year. Try this! Lightly cut back an 8" hanging pot in late September and pot it up into the next size pot (10" in my case), then when that pot fills with roots, (around January time) pot it on into a 12" or 14" basket. Such a simple way, but what a basket!

Without Heat: This way of growing a hanging pot or basket also makes use of a plant grown by the 'Multi-Plant' method but the plant will, of course, have to be overwintered in some way (see chapter 10). If your intentions are to try this method, and I would suggest that you do, follow this advice:

- Do not overpot your plant in its first season, flower it in a 4¼" or 5" half pot.

- In late September lightly cut it back to leave a good overhang of growth and pot it straight up into a 6" hanging pot. Overwinter it whichever way you choose — frost free and never, ever, let the compost go completely dry.

- Once winter is over and your plant is showing signs of growth check to see how the roots are getting on. When the pot is nicely filled with roots pot straight into an 8" hanging pot. Pinching out, etc., should be done as in Method One.

Growing a Standard

One of the main attractions of growing fuchsias is that they can be trained into almost any shape, with perhaps the most pleasing form of training being the Standard.

If you intend growing a Standard for your own pleasure it can be grown on any length of stem. However, if you wish to exhibit one there are certain rules with which you must comply. Here are the British Fuchsia Society rules on stem lengths.

- Full Standard: Stem length 30" to 42" in any size pot.
- Half Standard: Stem length 18" to 30" in any size pot.
- Quarter Standard: Stem length 10" to 18" in any size pot.
- Mini Standard: Stem length 6" to 10" in a 5¼" maximum size pot.

Note: Stem length is measured from the surface of the compost to the point where the lowest set of branches join the stem.

You can grow a cutting of almost any cultivar (some seem to do better grown as Standards) into a Standard but for the Full and Half Standard it is usual, but not essential, to choose one with a strong growing habit. The reason being that a good *'doer'* will have the vigour to more quickly attain the desired length of stem. For the Quarter and particularly the Mini you should choose a cultivar with small to medium flowers. The objective, whatever the size, should be to grow a well-balanced plant, i.e. size of pot, length of stem, size of head and flower, all coming together to give a sense of proportion.

So where do we begin? Well, first of all let me answer some popular questions on the subject of Standards.

Q. **Should I grow my Standard from a two leafed, or three leafed cutting?**

A. Personally, I always grow mine from a cutting with two leaves emerging from each node because my prime objective is to grow a Standard with a head of even growth. My reasons against a cutting with three leaves are: **a)** You would never grow a Standard of some cultivars if you waited until you found a cutting with three leaves.

b) Although you get extra growth in the head of a Standard from a three leafed cutting that growth is often uneven, particularly after the second pinch or stop.

Q. When is the best time to start a Standard?

A. If you have a heated greenhouse with a minimum temperature of around 45° Fahrenheit, or a windowsill in the home to grow them on, summer or early autumn is best. If not, it would be better to wait until spring.

Q. My whip is flowering. What should I do?

A. This is a problem that everyone who grows Standards encounters fairly frequently and the question *'What should I do?'* can be answered in several ways depending on what stage the *'whip'* (the name used for a Standard before the head is formed) has reached: **a)** If the whip has only reached about half the desired height there is, at this point, no real need to worry. Just make sure that the plant is not allowed to become potbound and is kept in reasonable light and a minimum growing temperature of 45° Fahrenheit in the hope that the plant will grow through its flowering stage and start to develop sideshoots. **b)** On the other hand if the whip has reached the stage where your chosen stem height has been reached and it is still flowering you do have a problem. The situation is not ideal but you have a decision to make. You either have to take the growing tip out at its present height and hope that branches break evenly from the top leaf joints when they finish throwing buds. Or, you accept that it will be taller than you want and allow it to grow through the flowering phase until sufficient new shoots develop to form the head.

Q. Why does my Standard come into flower before I have formed the head?

A. There are many reasons why the *'whip'* flowers early. Two points that may help to prevent it happening are: **a)** Try taking summer cuttings. The reason that spring cuttings often flower early is a natural one. Fuchsias are long daylight flowering plants and it is in their nature to flower in the summer months. By taking summer cuttings (use the perlite and water method — see page 19), even if they are in bud when you take them, you grow the whip up through the lowering daylight levels of autumn and winter, creating the height you require during the time when fuchsias don't normally flower. **b)** Never allow the plant to become potbound until the head is formed.

Right, lets get down to growing our Standard. I begin by placing a nicely rooted, even growing young plant into a 2½" pot, moving it to the next size *(I pot up from 2½" to 3" – 3" to 4" – 4" to 5", etc. — this larger jump in pot sizes, compared to when I am growing a bush, is to try and ensure that the root doesn't become restricted.)* when the roots first start to show at the edge of the pot. At *NO* stage let the young plant become potbound.

When the whip reaches about 5" in height insert a split cane, a few inches longer than the plant, alongside the stem. Then place a loose tie around stem and cane at every pair of leaves, changing the cane for a longer one as the plant grows. From this stage on you should start turning the plant every few days to maintain even growth. Whilst doing this, check that the ties remain loose, for just one tie cutting into the stem can disfigure it permanently.

Note: My method of tying during the development of the whip is to use short lengths of 2 ply garden twine which, after placing around stem and stake, I loosely tie with a single knot. It is then simply loosened by wiggling one end of the twine.

It is important to retain the leaves on the stem (they act as the plants lungs and usually grow quite large to compensate for the loss of leaves on sideshoots) as you continue to grow the whip up the cane. You should also decide what height of Standard you are going to grow, as it is at this time that you should start to remove sideshoots to keep the plant growing upwards.

As you require six or more sets of branches for a Full Standard and three or four for a Mini, it is wise to keep that amount of sideshoots at the top of the whip all the time it is growing. Start by removing any below the lowest pair of your chosen number, and then only take out the next lower set after a new pair appear at the top. Continuing to do this as the plant develops will ensure that even if the growing tip is damaged, or starts to develop flower buds before the required height is reached, you will have sufficient branches to form a head. These short Standards can be used as spot plants in the garden or for adding height to your greenhouse display.

When the stem reaches the required height, carefully remove the growing tip. The sideshoots that you left in at the top of the whip will now start to develop. These should be stopped, using a Mini Standard with four sets of branches as an example, when the bottom two pairs have three sets of leaves, the next set up two and the top pair one. Gradually shaping and building up the head as you would a bush plant. All that you are trying to do is to grow a bush on top of a long stem.

Some final points are:

- You should only remove leaves from the stem when the head has developed sufficient leaf area to sustain the plant.

- You should make sure that your Standard is securely staked. I use a garden cane or dowelling of a suitable diameter, and long enough to come right through the head so that it can be used to support branches.

- If you prefer, as I do, Standards of reasonable height (10" to 15" of bare stem) take your cuttings at any time during late June, the whole of July and August or even early September to have flowering plants for the following summer.

Note: These plants should be kept growing on in a temperature of around 45° Fahrenheit during their first winter.

Fuchsias in the Garden

Fuchsias, used as annual bedding plants or hardy perennials are a most useful plant for the garden. They flower almost continually from early summer until the autumn frost cuts them down. Having just mentioned that they can be used as a perennial plant I think I should say a few words on the hardiness of fuchsias at this stage. The first thing to get straight in our minds is that although many fuchsia cultivars are sold as being hardy, this is not exactly true as even those that have become well established can be killed in a severe winter. It is essential that even the hardiest of them are planted out correctly if they are to have a chance of becoming a permanent part of the garden.

As to which of the thousands of different cultivars available should be termed hardy, my own experience of planting out a wide range of fuchsias shows that it pays to experiment. Some of the so called *SOFTER* types that I have tried have been very successful indeed, which proves the point I am trying to make — a cultivar that needs protection in one part of the country may well be hardy in another — so don't be afraid of trying plants that you may already have in your collection. Many cultivars not thought of as hardy, could well turn out to be hardy for you. My advice is be adventurous, you will get some lovely surprises.

The points that you should look for in a good hardy are that not only should it come through winter, but also that it should start to flower in June, July or early August. It is of little use if the first flowers only start to appear in September, the first frosts of autumn could have appeared by then and that would be the end of your fuchsia, for that year anyway. Plants that flower too late in the season should be replaced.

If you are thinking of planting fuchsias in the garden for the first time, it is necessary for me to tell you about:

Conditions: The first thing to remind you of are the conditions that fuchsias require if they are to grow well. They would prefer to be planted in a position that faces east, north or west, rather than south. In fact fuchsias will add colour and grow very well in parts of the garden that get very little sun. Their other main requirement, which they should get in the garden anyway, is plenty of humidity.

The next stage is to decide whether you are going to use them solely as annual bedding plants, or plant them out permanently as hardy perennials. Let us now go through the two options:

Bedding Out: Once you are sure that all fear of frost has gone you can bed out fuchsias of all types, including Standards. Mature plants that you intend to lift before winter, especially those in clay pots, can be planted complete with pot if you wish, just make sure that the surface of the rootball is covered by about three inches of soil. Planting them out this way makes it easier to lift them in the autumn. All young plants should be planted bare rooted. You must remember that young plants, and most certainly Standards, unless you are prepared to lose them, should be lifted and stored before the frosts of winter arrive.

Note: Although I mentioned that you can plant fuchsias out complete with pot I prefer to remove it before planting. My reason for saying that is without the pot it is obviously much easier for the rootball to take up moisture from the surrounding soil, and it is not too much of a problem in autumn to cut off some of the roots to pot it up for storage.

Hardy Perennials: There are several points that you should consider if you wish to plant fuchsias out permanently:

Position: It is most important that you choose a position that is not in a frost pocket or tends to get waterlogged. It would also, as I have said before, be preferable if it could be in any aspect other than south.

Size of Plant: To give them a good start you should use well rooted plants from at least a 4" pot, but second year plants in 5" or 6" pots would be preferable.

When to plant out: The time to plant out is when all signs of frost have gone, because it is most important that the plants have a long growing season in which to develop a good root system. You would be taking a risk if you planted your fuchsias out after the end of June.

Planting out: Although fuchsias do not seem to be too fussy about the type of soil they grow in, they prefer to be planted in one that contains plenty of humus. The main aim when planting out is to protect the root system from frost. I would suggest that you make a saucer shaped depression before you dig the hole, this will level out during summer to give the root extra protection. When digging the hole make it deep enough so that the top surface of the rootball will be about three inches below soil level. Also, make it wide enough to allow you to incorporate some peat and perlite in the soil. These are added to encourage the roots to move out of the peat based compost, in which most pot fuchsias are grown, and into the soil. After removing the plant from its pot, take a split cane and gently scrape down the root several times. Again this is done to encourage the roots to branch out after planting — *see the end of the chapter for my latest thoughts on this subject.* Firm the plant well in to prevent wind damage and finish off by giving it a good watering.

Your fuchsias will require attention at various times during the seasons of the year:

Summer: Fuchsias planted from pots and especially those planted with their pot, will require watering and feeding until they become established.

Two of the worst pests that attack fuchsias in the garden are Capsid Bug and Thrips. These insects inject a poison into the growing tip of the shoots whilst feeding on the plant, damaging and distorting them to such an extent that it can prevent flowering. The main problem with both these pests is that damage is done before you are aware that they have attacked your plants. The best way I know of combating them is to start a course of preventative treatment. Spray the plant several times, using a range of suitable insecticides, as soon as they are in good leaf so that you kill them before they have a chance of devastating your plants. Whilst on the subject of pests, don't forget to check for Greenfly and Whitefly throughout the season and spray with insecticide when needed.

Note: To prevent wind damage, Standard fuchsias that you plant out must be supported by a stake that should be long enough to support not only the stem but also the head.

Autumn: Do *NOT* cut back the branches of your fuchsias when you are tidying up the garden. The cut stems become hollow, allowing water to seep down into the crown of the plant which frost could then damage. It is advisable to protect the crown of the plant with a mulch of bark or something similar as an added precaution against frost damaging the root system during winter.

Spring: In a normal winter most, if not all of the top growth of your fuchsias will be cut down by frost. New growth (on which the plant flowers) will, because the fuchsia is a shrub, come at or below ground level. The time to start removing the old dead wood is at the beginning of

May when, if you scrape away some of the mulch, you should see new growth emerging from the base of the plant. It is now that you should cut last year's growth back to one or two inches above the ground.

Occasionally, after a mild winter, you will find that new growth will start quite high up on the branches. In years like this you have the choice of either cutting them hard back or giving them a trim. If you decide to do the latter, remember that some cultivars are quite vigorous and can make four feet of growth in a season. This type of plant can easily get out of hand if not pruned back fairly hard. Once spring is under way and your fuchsias are starting to grow, give them a top dressing of a fertiliser such as Growmore or Vitax Q4 to help give them the vigour to keep flowering through to the autumn frosts.

Hardy Plants using the Multi-Plant Method: By using the Multi-Plant method you can easily and very quickly produce large plants for the garden. Plants started off in August or September easily make 5" pots by the following June, ready for planting out as soon as the fear of frost has past. These plants must of course be grown on through winter but they do not need too much heat (around 40° to 45° Fahrenheit would be warm enough), potting them on and stopping them whenever required.

When compared to the traditional way of planting out older plants in the garden, this way is startling. No more scratching the roots to encourage them to move into the soil. No more incorporating peat or perlite into the soil to help roots move from the peat based compost the plant is growing in to the soil of the garden. Because the young roots are growing towards the wall of the pot, they continue to grow sideways straight into the soil. You have to see for yourself the results of using a plant raised by this new method compared to an older pot plant that has had it's roots continually going round and round a pot for several years.

Note: Using Multi-Plants has changed my thinking on having permanent fuchsias in the garden. The quality and vigour of Multi-Plants and my enjoyment in producing them has meant that I am not too fussed if they do not survive the winter. I now prefer to have plants that I know will give me a great display, rather than accepting something that may have been badly damaged by the frosts. I also have variety in my garden instead of looking at the same old thing each summer. Just a thought!

Fuchsias in the Home

Why do flowers drop off my fuchsias? This question is often asked by someone who recently bought a plant for the home. The answer is simple, it is caused by a change of environment. A fuchsia plant in flower just cannot cope with the dry atmosphere prevalent in most homes, after living all its life in the humid conditions of a nursery. A plant faced with this sudden change in conditions will invariably drop buds, flowers and in extreme cases even its leaves. If this problem has happened to you the best remedy is to place the plant somewhere with more humidity in the atmosphere, perhaps a shady part in the garden would be best, until it recovers.

Although fuchsias do not make the best of pot plants for the home they can, if you pay attention to some simple points, be grown with some success. If, for instance, you know that fuchsias like cool, shady conditions, you will realise that they would prefer to be on a north or north-east window ledge, rather than one facing south. If you also know that they like humid conditions, you will provide them with a tray or large plant pot saucer filled with grit or small pebbles. By keeping the grit moist, but not so wet that the pot is standing in water, you will allow the plant to live in its own micro-climate of humidity. As an extra aid to providing humidity your fuchsias would also benefit from a fine mist spray each morning, and even more often on warm days. However, be careful when spraying flowering plants as the flowers easily mark.

By far the best method to use if you want to have flowering fuchsias in your home is to grow plants raised from your own cuttings, or obtain young unflowering plants from a nursery or garden centre. You will find that by growing these young plants on to maturity in the same environment in which they are to flower will have solved the problem of falling flowers.

Start to feed your plants regularly from early spring with a plant food that has slightly more Nitrogen than Potash, changing over to a balanced feed, or one that has slightly more Potash than Nitrogen, once flower buds start to form.

Do not overwater your plants. Like most pot plants, fuchsias do not like to have permanently wet feet. Let the compost nearly dry out before rewatering. Here are four helpful hints that will help you to tell when your plants need watering:

- **Weight of Pot:** Notice the difference in weight between a well watered plant and one that requires watering.

- **Colour of Compost:** Composts based on soil or sphagnum (Irish) moss peat are dark when wet and tend to turn a lighter colour as they dry out.

  Note: I always raise the foliage to see the colour of the compost before watering, or if that is not possible I look at the compost through the drainage holes in the bottom of the pot. Dependent on what I see I then do the following: a) If the compost is light-brown in colour I give the plant a full watering. b) If it is medium-brown I give it sufficient water to take it through the day. c) If it is dark in colour I do not water. The art in watering is to give the plant sufficient water to thoroughly moisten the compost without excess pouring out through the drainage holes.

- **By Touch:** Place your finger on the surface of the compost. If it is wet it will feel cooler to your finger than it will if it is on the dry side.

- **Foliage:** On a healthy plant you can also tell by the feel of the foliage. If the leaves are turgid the plant does not need watering, if they feel limp then it does. Foliage also changes colour when it starts to dehydrate due to lack of water.

Do not be discouraged by any setbacks that may occur. Try moving your plants around the home to find the most suitable place. Remember, as cool as possible, good light with protection from strong sunlight, and humidity, these are the conditions that fuchsias thrive on in their natural habitat. So if you, to the best of your ability, create these conditions in the home you will I am sure have much more success with your fuchsias.

Further thoughts on Fuchsias in the Home

If you put your mind to it your home can be a means of extending and improving your enjoyment of growing fuchsias. All that you need to do is make some space available during the winter months for overwintering mature plants or propagating new ones. So many of the ideas that I have developed for growing fuchsias are perfect for the person that does not have the benefit of a heated greenhouse. Let me give you just a few of my thoughts, others may come to you as you read this book.

- Mature plants can be overwintered in so many ways — in an unheated spare room, in the loft, cellar, porch, conservatory, etc. Just remember the two important points that must be achieved if fuchsias are to be successfully brought through winter, they should be kept frost free and the compost *MUST NEVER, EVER,* be allowed to completely dry out.

- With the advent of Multi-Planted fuchsias you can, and perhaps should have young plants in all stages of development as you approach winter. Remember, with this method of cultivation, this years small plants become next years large plants, and as they gradually develop through the winter months they can give you crop after crop of lovely soft tip cuttings.

- Next years new Standards can be grown on the windowsill from 'whips' produced by the Perlite and Water method of propagation (see page 19) or better still from cuttings taken from the much softer growth of your multi-plants when you pinch them out.

- Marvellous pot plants and hanging pots can be produced in the house by using the *'Coffee Jar'* or any other method of propagation that you use for taking cuttings. Once rooted and hardened off grow the young plants on as multi-plants.

- Try this idea! Root cuttings on the windowsill and when rooted move them into a much cooler place, i.e. porch, conservatory or even a cold greenhouse to harden off and grow on. Just take care in frosty periods to either cover with horticultural fleece or bring them into the house.

The message that I am trying to get across to anyone who hasn't the luxury of a heated greenhouse is that *YOU CAN*, if you put your mind to it, continue with your fuchsia hobby through the winter months. You may try some things and not succeed but there is no shame in that, the great shame would be not to have tried at all.

Overwintering Fuchsias

Bringing plants safely through winter is perhaps the greatest problem faced by growers. This chapter begins by dealing with traditional methods, continues with my own adaptation of tradition, then finishes with an entirely different approach using the Multi-Plant technique. The latter may seem to contradict what has gone before, but is simply explained by saying that traditional methods are usually for plants with ripe wood and could be several years old. The Multi-Plant method, however, deals with plants that although they may be large, are in fact quite young and should be kept gently growing on during the winter period.

Let me start by stating the two main requirements that mature fuchsias need to bring them safely through winter:

- They should be kept frost free.

- The compost *MUST NEVER* be allowed to become completely dry.

In winter, fuchsias can be stored anywhere that will ensure the above two points are maintained. I have heard of them being stored successfully in sheds, garages, cellars (they do not require light if they are fully dormant), lofts, etc. They can also be buried in moist peat or in trenches in the greenhouse or garden.

I can recommend the methods listed below as successful ways of bringing your plants through this difficult period, but before deciding which method you wish to use the next step will be to divide your plants into two groups

- **Young Plants:** Plants that have started life as cuttings in midsummer and autumn, and any other plants in which the growth is still soft will have to be grown on in normal light and gentle warmth.

- **Mature Plants:** All plants on which the growth has ripened can be overwintered by using any of the following methods:

Preparation: I usually start to prepare my plants for winter during October, although you can delay this if you wish to hang on to the last flowers of the season. By this time they are usually showing signs of needing a rest, and there could also have been that early frost. This first frost can be useful. If you have plants in the garden that you intend to protect, a slight frost will help them to shed their leaves. In fact, some growers purposely let their plants have a frost to help with defoliation before housing them for winter. There is just one point to beware of if you leave your fuchsias out to be frosted, and that is although a September or early October frost is usually a slight one (do watch the weather forecasts just in case), if the first frost doesn't occur until later it could be so severe that it could cause plant damage. So do take care.

My first stage of preparation is to prune the plants back by about a third. This usually leaves one or two sets of leaf joints above the plants last stop. Do not cut your plants back too hard at this time of year as fuchsias, like roses, can suffer from dieback. It is far safer to leave sufficient growth to enable you to give a final prune in spring when the sap is rising and new shoots start to appear. The next task is to cut off all the leaves (do not pull). This may seem an onerous task, but it is an important part of winter preparation. There are several reasons why:

- By removing the leaves you also remove unwanted pests and diseases.
- The plants can be placed closer together.
- You will not have leaves yellowing and falling off the plants to cause possible disease problems.
- This is the most important reason, it enables you to see the surface of the compost, making it easier to judge when plants need watering.

Having prepared the plants we can now look at various methods of overwintering them.

Any Frost Free Area: As I mentioned earlier, fuchsias in pots or plants lifted from the garden and boxed or potted up can be stored anywhere that frost does not penetrate. If they are kept cold (not below freezing) enough to go fully dormant they do not need light. Follow these points and you should bring your plants safely through to spring.

- Prepare your plants for their winter rest as above.
- To save room they can be placed close together on their sides, although I prefer to keep them upright. Standards can be laid down, as sap more readily runs along to the head in that position. Having said that, it would be safer if you could keep your Standards somewhere that has a temperature of around 45° Fahrenheit.

- Check your plants frequently to ensure that the compost has not become dry. More plants die from dehydration in winter than are ever lost from frost damage.

- I water any plant, using *TEPID* water, when the compost shows signs of becoming dry and is perhaps shrinking a little from the wall of the pot. I give sufficient water to moisten it, then wait (it could be several weeks) until the compost is nearly dry again before rewatering.

- Regularly turn plants that are laid on their sides to keep the sap flow even.

Partially Burying: This is the method that I would use if I did not have a heated greenhouse as the head of the plant is left uncovered. It is an ideal way of overwintering your bush or shrub fuchsias in the cold (lined with polythene) greenhouse, although it would be dangerous to try and over-winter Standards in this way. All you need is a supply of moist peat and some boards wide enough to make an area that will be deeper than the height of the pots. After preparing the plants, place them upright inside the space bounded by the boards. After making sure that the rootball is moist, fill in between and over the top of the pots until they are covered by about three inches of peat. I would suggest that you cover the head of the plant with several layers of horticultural fleece (available from most garden centres) whenever frost is imminent. The points in favour of this way of overwintering fuchsias are: **a)** By burying the pot you virtually ensure that you will not lose your plants from dehydration or frost damage to the root. **b)** The head of the plant being uncovered means that growth, when it starts in spring, will be natural and short jointed.

Completely Burying: Fuchsias can be safely stored for the winter by completely burying them if you follow this advice. All plants must have ripe wood, the foliage removed and the rootball moist. There are several methods, so I will describe them separately:

- **A Trench in the Garden or Greenhouse:** Dig a trench in part of the garden or greenhouse border that is not too wet, sufficiently deep so that the plants, when laid on their sides, will be covered by at least six inches of soil. After cutting back the heads of the plants to manageable proportions, prepare them as above and place them on their sides (with or without their pots) on the bottom of the trench, Standards included. Cover them with a piece of fine mesh plastic netting to make it easier to unearth them in spring, then gently fill in the trench. Finally, mark the position of the trench so that you will be able to dig them up again without damage.

- **Peat in an Outbuilding:** Make an enclosed area at the end of your garage or shed (polystyrene trays from a florists' shop can be used for the bottom and sides), and fill to a depth of three inches with moist peat. Place the prepared plants on their sides, then completely bury them to a depth of several inches with more peat.

- **Plants in Baskets or Hanging Pots:** These can be stored individually. All you need is a cardboard box several inches larger than the plant, a plastic bin liner and some moist peat. Line the box with the liner and put at least three inches of peat in the bottom. Place the prepared basket or pot in the bag and fill around and over the plant with several inches of peat. Close the neck of the bag and keep in a dry place.

Moderately Heated Greenhouse: I have always found it worthwhile to heat my greenhouse in winter. In the past, as an exhibitor, I could not afford to lose plants that may have taken years to develop. Now, as you will see later in this chapter, the Multi-Plant method of keeping plants growing on (without using any more heat) through the winter truly gives me an all the year round hobby.

Let me begin by describing the conditions in which my plants will be overwintered. I use a glass to ground 12ft by 8ft greenhouse which is lined with polythene to retain heat and prevent plants from being frosted through the glass. I use an electric fan heater fitted with an external rod thermostat to heat the greenhouse. With the thermostat placed amongst the plants at bench height I do not find electric more expensive than other types of heating. The points that I find in favour of heating by electric are: **a)** It only comes on when needed. **b)** You maintain a more even temperature. **c)** It helps to keep a drier atmosphere.

My main objective regarding the amount of heat I require is based on the quality of daylight available. It is pointless having too much heat in the greenhouse if it means that light levels are going to cause growth on plants to elongate, when what we should be looking for is compact growth. The temperature that I find to be about correct is between 42° and 45° Fahrenheit. Below that temperature you stand the risk of frost getting into the greenhouse, causing plant damage, before the heater can lift the temperature. Keeping the temperature much above 45 degrees leads to elongated growth and a much higher heating bill. Those are the conditions in which my plants will be living for the winter months, now let me tell you how I look after them during this period:

- My plants are prepared for their rest as previously described.

- Although plants do not go fully dormant they are in a state of rest, and this I tend to encourage because I want any growth that occurs to be short jointed.

- Every two or three days, more often in sunny periods, I check to see if any plant needs watering.

- I do not feed my plants during the winter, this is left until they show signs of life in spring.

- Each weekend I examine them for possible problems. I also turn each plant by a third before replacing it on the staging.

These tasks are continued until spring when hopefully, except for a little of the inevitable dieback on some cultivars, I will have successfully brought my plants through another winter. The money it has cost me has been well spent. For not only have I saved my plants for another season, I have also had untold hours of pleasure in the greenhouse during the worst part of the year.

If you haven't tried overwintering fuchsias before, preferring to go out and buy fresh plants each year, let me say that there is only so much growth that you can get from a young plant bought in spring. The full potential of a fuchsia will only be achieved by bringing it through the winter and growing it on for at least a second year.

REPOTTING — an improved method for you to try:

I have been experimenting with a method of cultivation I simply call '*REPOTTING*', and I can now tell you that it has helped me bring my mature fuchsias (plants with ripe wood) through winter with less of the usual problems. Let me explain my reasons for developing this method.

Overwintering fuchsias successfully is not the easiest of things to achieve, even with the aid of a heated greenhouse. The temperature level of just over 40° Fahrenheit that I keep is sufficient to keep the plants ticking over but not enough to create much root growth in the old compost in which they are growing. This has meant that I have had quite a lot of die-back on some cultivars, some problems with Vine Weevil grubs, and plants being damaged (leaves turning a reddish colour) by the sun in the early months of the year. My reasoning led me to think that if plants were gradually making fresh roots during this period they would be less susceptible to the problems just mentioned. The easy way to achieve this would have been to pot them up into fresh compost prior to winter setting in, but this I did not want to do as I much prefer to use the next larger size pot in springtime. I will describe my solution to the problem in the following stages:

- The time to do this is any time after the flowering season is over, perhaps from late September or early October. I have even *REPOTTED* them in early January with equally good results.

- All that you need is some fresh compost and a supply of clean pots.

- I will deal with a plant that started life in spring and was flowered in a 3½" pot, but of course the same treatment can be done to plants in other size pots because all that you are doing is replacing them in a similar sized pot to the one in which they have been growing.

- Prune the plant back as described at the top of page 59 but do not defoliate at this stage as it is better to wait until the plant has recovered from the disturbance.

- Remove the plant from its pot and with a sharp knife (I use an old bread knife) cut a quarter of an inch off the outer edge of the compost, to the shape of the pot, and the same amount off the bottom. The aim is to reduce the rootball so that it fits into a 3" pot. With plants in larger sized pots reduce the rootball to fit the next size smaller, e.g. 5" to 4".

- Take a clean 3½" pot and make a 3" form (see page 34 — using the *FORMER* method) with my multi-purpose soilless compost mix (see bottom of page 11).

- All that you have to do now is place the plant into the form you have just made and firm it in.

The beauty of this method is that you do minimal damage to the rootball, yet place fresh compost for the roots to grow into without changing the pot size. The plant then goes into winter making roots, feeding itself from the fresh compost as it does so, the result is a fitter plant that does not seem to suffer too much from dieback, breaks readily in spring and is better able to withstand a possible attack from our *FRIEND* the Vine

Weevil. With the temperature in the greenhouse kept at the above levels I do not find growth excessive, on the contrary, it is healthy and short jointed.

Multi-Plants in the Winter Months: During my development of multi-planting fuchsias I have started to seriously question traditional methods of fuchsia cultivation, and the way we overwinter them is certainly one. I think you will agree there are enough bare leafed trees outside without filling our greenhouses up with them as well. My experience with the *REPOTTING* method showed me that fuchsias came through winter far better if they were making root. My advice now, whether you have a heated greenhouse or not, is to evolve a method that allows your Multi-Plants to keep growing on, no matter how slowly.

The method that I have evolved means that the great majority of my plants see only one winter. They are started off at any time of year that cutting material is available, those that began life between November and early March (I do not count this as the first winter) are invariably kept to a maximum 5" sized pot during their first flowering season. These plants, if I wish them to become much larger plants the following year, will be potted up around October or November. If I wish to keep the growth more compact and not have such large plants I use the *REPOTTING* method where I remove a small amount of root area and replace the plant in the same size pot. Plants in smaller pots are always potted up into the next size pot prior to winter. I only take a few plants through a second winter for baskets or patio tubs, so the maximum length of time that I keep my multi-plants is two winters and three summers.

Note: A more detailed explanation of my winter/spring multi-plant culture follows at the end of the next chapter.

Fuchsias in Early Spring

Now, although this chapter will take us into spring and all the tasks that will bring there is still, to begin with anyway, plenty of cold weather with which to contend. And although my Multi-Plant method has meant that I have almost completely changed my techniques in growing fuchsias I will begin by dealing with the more traditional methods of culture, then give my more modern thoughts on how I grow my plants through this most interesting period. However, whichever way you choose to grow your fuchsias, spring, if you are not careful, can also be a time of disaster with plants being damaged by frost, disease or pests.

Let me now describe on a month by month basis how I care for my fuchsias during this critical period, starting with plants that have been brought through winter in a dormant or semi-dormant condition.

January is the month when, in the heated greenhouse, the first signs of movement start to show on pot plants overwintered in the traditional way. The shortest day is behind us and although it is not too noticeable, the length and quality of daylight are starting to improve. During the early part of the month I continue with the weekly winter task of examining and turning my plants. Looking mainly for any signs of trouble, such as plant material showing symptoms of Botrytis (Grey Mould), Rust, Vine Weevil or sap sucking pests on the undersides of old or new leaves. The task of keeping fuchsias clean from pests and diseases during the summer months starts *NOW* with these weekly inspections. For instance, the first Whitefly to be seen can simply be squashed between finger and thumb, and any sign of disease can be dealt with long before it gets out of hand.

One other necessary duty at this time of year is, of course, watering. So twice a week, more often in bright sunny spells, I check through my plants to look for any in which the compost has turned a lighter shade of brown. With my compost being based on sphagnum (Irish) moss peat the fact that it changes to a paler colour as it dries tells me not only whether a plant needs watering, but also almost how much water to give that plant. I find that by allowing each plant to go towards the dry side (be careful not to leave them too long in this state) before rewatering helps to prevent the premature growth that sometimes occurs during mild winters. The amount of water I give each plant at this time of year is much less than I would give them when they are in full leaf, but is sufficient to moisten *ALL* the rootball. I find that watering in this manner keeps my plants ticking over.

Note: If the compost has dried out to the state that it has started to shrink a little from the wall of the pot it MUST be watered immediately.

One other point to note is that I do not feed my plants at all during the colder months. Liquid feeding *MATURE* fuchsias when the temperature is below 50° Fahrenheit is not only a waste of money it is also unnecessary. Plants that are in a state of rest do not require feeding, and unused salts from the feed could build up in the compost to cause possible future problems.

Later in the month we should start to see a marked improvement in light levels, and on sunny days a general rising of greenhouse temperatures. The usual advice on these sunny mornings, and something I certainly used to do (see note below), is to start spraying the bare branches of rested plants with *TEPID* water. This is done to encourage new growth by softening the wood of the plant. I always used a *mister* for these early sprays because it is important that the plants dry off before nightfall.

Note: With reference to misting the plants with tepid water — I now find that this is unnecessary as my plants break into new growth quite naturally on their own, without any interference from me. The reason they break on their own is because I endeavour not to get the wood of the plant too ripe during the summer months. It is important NOT to overfeed fuchsias with potash — see chapter on feeding.

February is the month when things really get started. Much more time will have to be made available to do the many jobs that need doing if we are to give our plants a good start to their growing season. The main tasks ahead of us at this time are Pruning, Potting Down and Potting Up. Before doing any of these things, however, I must tell you that I think it is important not to disturb any plant unless it is showing signs of growth. I find that damage can occur on plants disturbed too much when they are dormant. I also do not believe in trying to rush plants into growth by providing extra heat. In my experience it is daylight length, and not warmth, that triggers them into growth. Any plant that is allowed to grow naturally is usually far better than one that has been forced in some way.

Pruning: The final spring pruning of my plants is done mainly in late January and early February but can be done later if you do not provide them with winter warmth. It is something that must be done with great care because it so easy to spoil a plant. There are several guidelines that I use and I will list them before I describe how I go about this, for me anyway, pleasant task.

- Allowing the compost to nearly dry out before pruning helps to prevent sap bleeding from cut branches. Keeping them on the dry side (not too dry) for a few days afterwards will also help.

- Sap bleeding from the stems is usually the cause of Botrytis occurring after the leaves start to appear. If you look carefully at where the disease has started you will usually find that it is around the end of a cut stem. To help prevent Botrytis starting you may find it beneficial to dab some fungicide powder (one grower I know uses 'Copydex' – the carpet glue) on all the cut ends of stems. My own cure for Botrytis is to have plenty of air circulating around and through the plants.

- Do not prune a plant until signs of growth are noticeable.

- Do not prune back too hard.

- Do use sharp secateurs to make clean cuts.

- My method of pruning starts with an examination of the plant, taking in the general shape, type of growth and how far to cut it back. Whatever the plant's size, the main factor when pruning is to cut back the growth to a framework that will support the weight of foliage and flowers. My first year plants, and any that are going to be potted into a larger size pot, are invariably cut back to one pair of growing points above the previous years last pinch or stop. I do prune a little lower than this on cultivars with weak growth, but even then only cutting off enough to leave the plant with the essential *FIRM* framework. On older plants, where the size of the head in relation to the pot size would be too large, I do prune back to slightly harder wood so that the final size of the plant will be in proportion to its pot. Plants that do not break evenly after this treatment are used in the garden.

When pruning I start with the top branches, then shape outwards and downwards to the lower ones, so that the final shape is as near as possible symmetrical. Step back from time to time to check how you are getting on as it is so easy to take off more than you should. Do take care, remember, you can always take off a little more, but you can *NEVER* put any back.

Potting Down, or Potting Back as it is also called, is a term used to describe the removal of some of the old fibrous roots on pot grown plants before replacing them, using fresh compost, into a clean pot usually a size smaller than the original one. Potting down should be done just after the first signs of top growth, and before the start of too much root development. Remove the plant from its pot and tease away the old compost, taking care to do as little damage as possible to any fresh white roots that may be showing. If the plant is an old one with very thick mature roots, you may find it easier to place it back into a clean pot of a similar size to its original one. Then using a good quality compost that contains plenty of aeration and drainage materials (grit and perlite) repot the plant, taking note of the following points:

- If you notice any small grubs with brown heads and curled into a semi-circular shape (Vine Weevil grubs) when potting down, do make sure that you remove them all, otherwise they could destroy the plant by eating its roots.

- You can also improve the looks of a plant at this time by straightening it up in its pot, or even lowering it down to cover some of the bare stems that tend to occur on older fuchsias.

- Do make sure that the compost fills all the spaces around the roots. The use of a piece of split cane and frequent tapping of the pot helps to do this.

- After watering, shade the plant until it has recovered from the disturbance, then let it nearly dry out before rewatering.

- Pot up in the usual way when roots begin to fill the pot.

My own feelings on this aspect of fuchsia culture are mixed. I know that the great majority of growers find potting down successful and I do not want to put you off using this method, but my own experience of it has been far from satisfactory. Too many of my plants have been damaged, with branches dying back on some cultivars and the roots of others not recovering from the disturbance. The reason for this damage in my case is, I am sure, the lack of an area of shade in my south facing garden. When you think about it we are usually potting back our plants in February, which is the time of year when the sun starts to become quite hot through glass. Surely, it makes sense to think that if you cannot place the plants somewhere to recover until their roots start to grow again, they could well be damaged by sun drying up the young, tender growing shoots. The end result in my case has led to a lot of die back on some cultivars, and the complete loss of others. I know that I could put more shading on the glass to combat this problem, but it is far too early in the season to use anything other than light shade. One of the most important requirements at this time of year is good quality light to help keep the new growth on plants as short jointed as possible.

An alternative method for anyone who has had similar problems with potting down, is to try growing their plants on for at least a second year in the same compost. I will explain my procedure with any plant that I am not potting down (minimum 5" pot), or that I will not be potting up in the following points:

- Once growth starts, usually early February, I sprinkle the surface of the compost with calcified seaweed (50% of which is Calcium). This is done to add trace elements and to help sweeten the compost.

- In mid March I scrape off some of the old compost from the top of the pot, and replace it with fresh, before adding more calcified seaweed.

- Once growth is really underway I place a little base fertiliser on the surface of the compost, either Chempak Potting Base or Vitax Q4 is ideal.

- During the growing season I feed regularly with a liquid feed that contains a full range of trace elements, as well as the usual Nitrogen, Phosphates and Potash. Chempak have the perfect range of feeds for fuchsias. No.2. High Nitrogen, No.3. Balanced and No.4. High Potash. They also contain seven essential trace elements.

- Finally, a word of warning. If you are troubled with our FRIEND the Vine Weevil I would recommend that you revert to potting down so that the grubs can be removed.

- *Note: Although growing plants on for a second year in the same compost was an improvement on potting down for me, I would now recommend the use of the 'REPOTTING' method as described in the last chapter.*

Potting Up: I always wait until plants are growing well before starting to pot them up, usually during the months of March and April. One point to remember at this stage is that it is important to allow a plant that has been potted up to become potbound for it to flower well, so do not pot up too late in the season. Other points to note are:

- Always use clean pots.

- Do leave enough space at the top of the pot to allow for watering. Make allowance for the fact that the surface of the compost rises when the pot becomes packed with roots.

- If you have any intention of exhibiting your plants, do make sure that the pots you use are in good condition and of a type allowed within the rules of the show schedule.

Later in the month, on sunny mornings, I spray water between plants on the greenhouse staging. I do this to provide the humidity that all fuchsias need, but take care that you do not over do it at this time of year. Ideally, all moisture should dry out by nightfall. You should also ventilate the greenhouse whenever weather permits. It may also be necessary to provide some light shading at this time as the sun can easily cause plant damage if it is allowed to shine through clear glass.

March: Plants should be growing on quite strongly now that the daylight hours are lengthening. The lovely thing about this time of year is that new growth is usually short jointed, so do not miss the opportunity to take some cuttings.

You will be extremely fortunate if the new growth on your plants breaks evenly. I usually find with mine that I have to level it up. The longer shoots are cut back to bring them back into line with the general shape of the head, and those that are just emerging left untouched. The reason for this is that the retarded growth will be more evenly matched with the sideshoots on that just cut back. Stopping for shape each time, instead of at every pair or two pairs of leaves as is often recommended, will improve the general appearance of your plants. Other important tasks during this month are as follows:

Ventilation: Do continue with ventilating the greenhouse as often and as much as you are able.

Shading: Do watch out this month. The sun is getting stronger by the day. You *MUST* shade as necessary.

Note: If you are not quite sure of when to start to shade your plants keep an eye on the foliage. The leaves of a plant can tell you whether it is getting too much sun or not, e.g. The beautiful white, double flowered, cultivar 'Annabel' has lovely yellowy/green leaves when all is well, but if it starts to get too much sun the veins in the leaves start to turn red. Watch out also for foliage starting to get much harder than it was earlier in the year. By regularly handling your plants you soon get a feeling of what the foliage should feel and look like when it is growing well. The challenge of growing any plant to perfection in a pot is to notice when things are not going quite right, then rectify them before they do any permanent damage.

Humidity: Progressively use more water (not so wet that plants take up water) on the staging aggregate during sunny spells. Remember, if the temperature in the greenhouse rises to damaging levels your plants will take less harm if the atmosphere is humid.

Pests and Diseases: Begin a regular spraying programme now to keep your plants clean. My golden rule on pests and diseases is — if your plants come through winter and spring clean you greatly reduce the chances of having problems later on.

April/May: Spring should be with us now and the temperature beginning to rise, so if you have overwintered your fuchsias by the *'Completely Burying'* method (see page 60) you should be thinking of bringing them out of store. Now that the days are beginning to warm up, plants that have been buried will have started into growth. Carefully lift them, taking care not to damage any of the white tender shoots as these are your new branches. Place them in a light but not too sunny area and the shoots will soon turn green. Cut them back to one pair of leaves above where the growth started and pot them into fresh compost. If you did not prune your plants back too hard before burying them you can cut back below the new shoots into riper wood.

Do remember to watch out for the weather forecasts each day as it would be a pity if, having safely brought your plants through winter, you lost them on the first frosty night. If you do not have a frost free area, you can give plants some protection by placing several layers of newspaper or 'Horticultural Fleece' over the branches.

Multi-Plants: It is January as I write these words and I can honestly say, looking at my plants, that it looks more like April or May. Almost all of my plants are in full leaf and some have even had their last stop (I want to see just how far I can stretch the flowering season). I look at the comparison of this method of fuchsia culture to the more traditional methods, where at this time of year I would only, hopefully, be seeing tiny new shoots emerging from the woody branches and think I have been living in the 'Dark Ages' — this method *HAS* to be the way forward for anyone interested in growing fuchsias.

Let me give you some pointers as to how I have adapted my knowledge of traditionally bringing fuchsias through winter and into spring to suit this completely new Multi-Plant approach to their culture. My thoughts throughout have been:

NEW APPROACH TO GROWING? — TRY NEW METHODS OF CULTURE!

- I take cuttings whenever they are available throughout the year. This means that I have pots of fuchsias at all stages of growth as I approach winter.

- Beginning in late September I start to prepare multi-plants that started life in the earlier months of the year and have flowered during the summer — these can be in pot sizes varying from 3½" to 5" — for the winter period. Each plant is treated individually and pruned lightly back (if the plant is in full fresh flower I delay pruning until it is past its best) to one pair of leaves above its last pinch or stop. This pruning is carefully done to leave, as near as possible, a symmetrical shape. Plants in 3½" or 4¼" pots are then potted up into the next size pot. I treat plants in 5" pots differently: **a)** If my intention is to grow the plant on to become a much larger plant next season it is potted on and continues to be potted on, whatever the month, whenever it nicely fills its pot with roots. **b)** On the other hand, if I wish to keep some sort of control on the plants size and have it in only a slightly larger pot the next season I use the *'REPOTTING'* method described in the last chapter. This cultural procedure places fresh compost around the roots without increasing the pot size — with either method plants immediately start to make fresh roots and continue to grow throughout the winter.

- Multi-Plants which started life during the summer and autumn months and have heads that are still being developed by pinching out are potted on until the pot size in which you intend to flower them is reached.

Note: Remember that there is no need to keep potting multi-plants up if you don't wish, many, if not all, of the small to medium flowered cultivars are quite happy retained and flowered in a 3½" pot.

- Because my plants are kept growing on, no matter how slowly, I continue to feed them (*10mm 'Maxicrop Original' plus 10mm 'Fisons Liquinure' per gallon*) at each watering during the winter and early spring period. This may at first seem an unwise thing to do, but when you think about it you are only watering perhaps once or twice a week at most, so this weak feed, I can assure you, just keeps them gently growing on.

Multi-Planting fuchsias is a cultural method that can be tailored to your needs. If you want to grow large plants, keep potting them on into big pots. On the other hand if you wish to put some constraint on the growth, don't pot them on as freely — it really is up to you. I now look at my plants and can't quite believe what I am seeing. The difference between growing one plant in a pot and growing many really has to be seen to be believed.

Exhibiting Fuchsias

I am writing this chapter on exhibiting fuchsias in the hope that it will encourage anyone who hasn't placed a plant on the showbench before to do so at their next local show.

Note: Please do not skip this chapter thinking that it is just about showing fuchsias as there is a great deal of information in it that will be of use to all growers.

Exhibiting fuchsias began for me soon after I joined South Lakeland Fuchsia Society at Kendal. Before then I had been growing and enjoying fuchsias for quite a few years, and thinking back I can remember that even then I tried to grow my plants into a nice even shape. This I am sure helped me when I was persuaded to enter some plants in the Fuchsia Section of the 1979 Lakeland Rose Show.

After going through the nerve-racking experience of staging my first plants, I returned to the marquee after judging to find that not only had I won the Novice Section, I had also picked up several more Firsts in the Open Classes. I still find it almost impossible to explain in words the elation and excitement that I felt. Needless to say I was hooked, and from that day on started to concentrate on trying to grow all my fuchsias to the high quality required for the showbench.

During the many years I spent as an exhibitor I gained a great deal of experience and developed many useful skills which I would now like to pass on to you. My reasons for doing this are to encourage anyone who hasn't entered a show before to do so, and also to help anyone who has only just started. If you are hesitant about exhibiting, I can assure you that after overcoming the initial nervousness of placing your first plant on the showbench, you will enjoy the experience and the winning of your first award card will give you a real thrill.

Here are some points that will help:

- Grow your plants with the intention of showing them. You will find that you will grow better plants and have more success if you have something to aim for, rather than looking around the greenhouse for something that might do on the day.

- If you grow your exhibition plants, particularly the bush shape, from a single plant it is essential that you choose cuttings that have leaves and sideshoots with even growth, as no one can make much out of an uneven plant.

- Although it is not quite as important to have cuttings of such even growth with the Multi-Plant method it is essential that the sizing of them is as even as possible. The main points required to grow symmetrical Multi-Plants are: **a)** The cutting material *MUST* be the soft growing tips of the plant and not the longer, more traditional type of cutting. **b)** The outer ring of cuttings should be as equal in size as possible, with the slightly larger or smaller ones in the middle. **c)** If you have rooted cuttings directly into the pot, do not forget that you can often improve that pot by transplanting (whilst the roots are still small) plants from the middle of the pot to the edge if it makes the outer ring of plants more even. **d)** Whenever you stop the plant, pinch out for shape, following the natural outline of the plant and letting any retarded growth catch up with the general shape of the plant before removing their growing tips.

- Do not overpot fuchsias grown from a single plant during their first season. Remember that there are classes for 3½" and 4" pots in most shows. I also feel that by not overpotting you build up a more compact framework to the plant, this will stand you in good stead in the following years of its life. With Multi-Plants you will have to evolve a system for when to start your plants for the different pot sizes. To give you a rough guide I grow 3½" or 4" pots in approximately 6 months. 5" pots between 9 and 15 months, and 6" pots in 18 to 20 months.

- Do remember that the next to the last stop is just as important as the final one. Count back the weeks from the show date to your final stop, then allow at *LEAST* four weeks before that for your penultimate stop. This is necessary to allow enough growth to develop for you to make your final one.

- If you haven't stopped a plant for show before, I would suggest that you first of all look to see if there are any signs of flower buds in the growing shoots of the plant. If you cannot see any, allow ten weeks for a single or semi-double cultivar, and about twelve weeks for a double. You can reduce the above times by at least two weeks if buds are showing.

75

Note: Because fuchsias grown by the Multi-Plant method do not drop their tiny buds, and flower for such a long period of time, it is much easier to time them for a show. Just make sure that they are in full flower for show day by stopping them a little earlier than you would for the more traditional single plant.

- It is advisable to make a note of the date of the last stop, and also the day when the plant is in full flower. This information will be a useful reference until you become familiar with the length of time a particular cultivar takes to flower from its last stop.

- After stopping your plant, go over it again during the next week to ten days to catch any shoots that you may have missed, and also any sideshoots that are progressing well in advance of the others. Then look closely at the emerging sideshoots, they should all be of a similar size. What you are trying to do is balance the growth so that the whole head of the plant flowers as evenly as possible.

- Do obtain and carefully study the show schedule.

- As most shows are judged to British Fuchsia Society Standards obtain a B.F.S. Judges & Exhibitors Handbook from your local Society or from the B.F.S. This, and the schedule for the show, will tell you the things that you may or may not do, for example, I have seen exhibitors disqualified from a class for not using the correct type of pot, and also for using two stakes to support the stem of a Standard. Yet the rules plainly state the type of pots that must be used, so, when you pot up your plants into their final pots make sure that they are of the right type, and that they are in good condition. In the case of the Standard with two stakes, the rules again plainly say that it may be supported by a *SINGLE* stake. Do check the rules carefully so that you do not get that dreaded note against your exhibit N.A.S. (not as schedule).

- Do not wait until the last minute to prepare your plants for the show. Much of what needs doing should be done at home in the days preceding the show, such as: **a)** Removing all yellow or damaged leaves. **b)** Cleaning debris, moss, etc. from the surface of the compost. **c)** Thoroughly clean the pots and replace any that have been damaged with one of the same make and size.

- Look round your plants at least a week before the show to see that they are pest and disease free. This will give you a little time to clear possible problems. Do *NOT*, on any account, take infected plants to the show.

- Do *NOT* be tempted to pot up, pot down, or dig a plant up from the garden to fill a class at the show. It simply is not worth it. It takes a long time to build up a good reputation as an exhibitor, a reputation that can be lost in an instant if you are caught cheating.

- Bees and Wasps badly mark flowers, keep them out of the greenhouse.

- Remove any flowers that open up to ten days before the show, they will be past their best on the day and will only drop pollen and nectar on the foliage if left on the plant. Flowers that start to open on or after that ten day period are left on the plant to develop. Carefully check over the plant the day before the show to remove dead flowers. A dead flower is one on which the pollen on the stigma has died.

- Make sure that the stem length of your plants conform to the rules.

- Bush Plant: Maximum length of stem 1½".

  Mini Standard: Minimum length 6" – Maximum length 10".

  Quarter Standard: Minimum length 10"   Maximum length 18".

  Half Standard: Minimum length 18" – Maximum length 30".

  Full Standard: Minimum length 30" – Maximum length 42".

- Do not send your entry form in too early. Wait until you are sure that you can fill the classes of your choice, but make certain that it gets to the Show Secretary by the specified date.

- There are several things that you should take with you to the show: **a)** Take more plant pot saucers than you need, they can be useful to raise a plant slightly in a multi-pot class so that visually they are more evenly matched. **b)** A pair of secateurs. **c)** A sharp knife. **d)** Some split canes. **e)** A mist sprayer — a fine mist will not mark your flowers, but it will freshen up the plant. **f)** A small piece of clean cloth which, when moistened, can be used to remove pollen and nectar from the leaves. **g)** Some white card to use if there are no official cultivar name cards at the show, and of course a pen.

- Water your plants the evening before the show. If it has been a warm day and you leave watering until the morning, they may be wilting and could take hours to recover.

- Do make sure that your plants travel to the show safely. Place them in concrete blocks, upturned cardboard boxes with holes cut in them, polystyrene flower pot trays, etc. — in fact anything that will stop them from falling over. Take note of how other exhibitors get their plants safely to the show.

- Arrive at the show in good time. First of all contact the Show Secretary to obtain your Exhibitor Cards. Do not hesitate to ask for assistance if you are exhibiting for the first time. Everyone, including the top exhibitors, will be only too pleased to help. Do make full use of the time available to you before judging to stage and dress your plants.

- Right! Now is the time to put the final touches to your plants. It has taken you at least all season to grow them, so do not let them down by simply dropping them on the bench and leaving everything to chance.

- This is the procedure I go through when putting my plants on the showbench: **a)** Find the position of the classes you have entered and place a plant pot saucer (the same colour as the pot) on the bench. **b)** Bring in your plants. **c)** Start to dress them by lifting all the flowers and buds on to the top of the foliage, trying to cover the whole plant evenly. **d)** Lift your plant and look inside it to check for any yellow leaves, debris on pots, etc. and place it back on the bench with its best side to the front. **e)** Clean pollen and nectar off the leaves. **f)** Step back and look at your plant from a distance, it is amazing just how much you can miss. **g)** Make out a cultivar name card. If you do not know the name of your plant write *'Name Unknown'*. Place your exhibitors card face downwards, and the name card face upwards in front of your exhibit. **h)** Give your plants a drop of water to make absolutely sure that they do not wilt before judging. **i)** Have one last look at your plants to make sure that you haven't missed anything, that you are in the right class, and that you have put the correct exhibitor and name cards in front of your plants.

Finally, do take part in your local show, I know you will enjoy the experience. You may not win an award, but by taking part you will have a feeling of satisfaction, you will also have helped to give pleasure to all who visit the show.

Feeding Fuchsias

Keeping fuchsias healthy within the confines of a pot after the nutrients in the compost have been used is a task that requires a skill that can take the beginner some time to acquire. It is so easy to overfeed and cause damage to the plant, or underfeed and not get the desired quality of growth. Explaining how and when to feed your pot or container grown plants in a simple way is not going to be easy. Perhaps the best way to pass on the knowledge I have gained over many years of growing fuchsias will be in a series of questions and answers. These will then, I hope, explain this very important part of fuchsia culture.

Q. **What do the letters N.P.K. mean?**

A. Any feed, whether it is in a bottle or a packet, has to have its analysis printed on the label. The letter 'N' stands for Nitrogen and promotes growth in the leaves and stems of the plant. 'P' is for Phosphates which feed the roots. Potash is represented by the chemical symbol 'K' and this element of feed helps to ripen the growth of plants, it also enhances flower colour.

Q. **What do the numbers under or by the letters N.P.K. mean?**

A. These numbers show you the ratio of fertilisers in the feed. For example, the numbers 1-1-1 under the letters N. P. K. tell you that it is a balanced feed containing equal parts of Nitrogen, Phosphates and Potash. The same type of feed could be marketed by a different manufacturer as 20-20-20. Don't be confused, the latter isn't a stronger feed, just another way of saying that it is a balanced feed. If the first number is higher than the last (25-15-15) it is called a high nitrogen feed, and when the numbers are reversed (15-15-25) it is called high potash.

Q. **What feed should I use?**

A. There is no universal feed with which to feed your plants if you wish to grow them to their best. Fuchsias in pots have differing needs depending on:

a) In what type of compost they are growing.

b) The season of the year.

c) Whether it is a cold wet summer, or a hot sunny one.

I know all this sounds complicated, but if you do not have the time to spare, or if you do not wish to try and give the plant what it needs, whenever it needs it, then feed right through the season with a balanced feed. When buying a feed, don't just look for one with the ratio of nutrients that you require, look also at how many trace elements there are in its makeup, then choose the one with the most.

Q. **When do you start to feed your plants?**

A. I will have to answer this question in two parts, dealing first with older plants, and then with young ones in their early stages of growth.

Mature Plants that have been brought through winter in a dormant or semi-dormant state need feeding with care in spring until they come fully into growth. It is far better to spray bare branches with clear TEPID water to encourage them into growth, rather than pouring food into a pot where the roots haven't started moving. My first feed of the year is usually given in early April. I water any plant that is showing signs of new growth with High Nitrogen feed, e.g. 3-1-1, (3 parts Nitrogen, 1 part Phosphates and 1 part Potash) at a quarter of the strength the manufacturer of the feed recommends. This weak feed is given again at weekly intervals depending on the temperature in which the plants are living. It is not good practice to feed plants if it is much below 50° Fahrenheit or if the roots have not started moving in search of food. Once the plant has really started to grow you can start to feed a little more, not with a stronger feed, but gradually more frequently with quarter strength feeds.

Young Plants are treated differently. I do not think it necessary to liquid feed plants when they are young, because they are continually being potted up into fresh compost that contains everything they need. I find that by allowing them to search for food, not only encourages root development, but also helps to keep growth compact. I begin to liquid feed only after a plant has been potted on into the pot in which it is going to live for the rest of the season.

Note: The above advice is for the traditional 'one plant in a pot' *method. You will probably already have noticed in earlier chapters that I start feeding Multi-Planted fuchsias quite early, and right through winter. This may seem to contradict what I have just said but the answer is simple, they are two entirely different methods of cultivation. The growth of the single plant needs to be as compact as possible to keep the branches close together. On the other hand, the Multi-Plant method produces so many branches that keeping compact growth hardly matters.*

Q.   **Why feed at a quarter strength?**

A.   Most plants prefer to have a frequent supply of weak feed, rather than a strong one at weekly intervals. The recommended method of feeding fuchsias is to use a quarter strength feed at every watering, but there are two comments on this subject that I would like to add at this stage:

a) If you have to water more than once a day use clear water for the second watering.

b) I think it better to quarter strength feed every other day in prolonged hot spells when you have to water your plants every day. This is to prevent overfeeding. Feeding your plants every day with a quarter strength feed means that you are pouring food into the pot at almost twice the makers recommendation. If feeding was to carry on at this rate for several weeks it could cause the balance of nutrients in the compost to be disturbed or even worse, damage to the roots.

Q.   **In spring, why do my plants produce flower buds instead of leaves?**

A.   Mature plants that have had a winter rest tend to do this if the wood of the plant is overripe. The usual cause of wood becoming too ripe is the over use of High Potash feeds during the previous season. Potash is an element of food that seems to be retained by the plant. If your fuchsias have this fault of producing flower buds instead of leaves and shoots, the answer to the problem is to use less Potash. Try using no more than a balanced feed on your plants right through the season, and if you have a very sunny garden you may even find

81

that the use of a High Nitrogen feed would be even better. Other symptoms of a plant that has too much Potash in its system are stunted growth, leaves smaller than is usual for that particular cultivar, and flowers that are not of full size.

Q. **What do you think of foliar feeds?**

A. Spraying a plant with foliar feed can be useful early in the season, but I do not think it necessary if the plant is growing on healthily in a good quality compost. Your plants will benefit, however, from a couple of sprays of Magnesium (Epsom Salts) at the rate of 1 ounce to the gallon later in the season, but do this before the flowers open to avoid marking them.

Other points on feeding are:

• Have a range of feeds with different nutrient ratios so that you can vary them as needed. Use one with more Nitrogen than Potash in the early months of the year, a balanced feed for mid-season, and one (dependent on the environment of your garden — *not too sunny*) with more Potash than Nitrogen when the plants come into bud.

• Your plants can tell you a lot about their feeding needs. Notice the condition of the foliage, and also the general growth of your plants. Large soft leaves, with growth that has no strength, tell you that the plants could do with some Potash to firm them up. If the leaves are small for the type of cultivar, the wood too ripe, and the growth stunted, then they would benefit from some extra Nitrogen. On the other hand, if the leaves and growth seem right for the plant, feed with a balanced feed.

• Be prepared to give the plants a feed or two of Potash if the growth becomes soft in long dull periods. Equally, in prolonged sunny spells give them a few feeds of Nitrogen if it becomes a little hard. If, like me, you have a very sunny garden with little or no shade you will probably find that the use of a High Potash feed causes your plants to become too hard. The reason for this is that the sun naturally ripens them (a popular name for Potash is liquid sunshine), so feeding fuchsias High Potash in a hot summer is not only unnecessary, it can cause the wood of the plant to become overripe.

- The blanket advice usual given on feeding fuchsias is to feed High Potash when flower buds first show in the tips of the shoots. For *ANYONE* with a south facing garden in a good summer it could be the worst advice they have ever had. I find that my plants do best by using a High Nitrogen feed (I now use Fisons Liquinure 8 – 4 – 4) throughout the season, only giving the occasional feed of balanced fertiliser in dull periods.

  Note: With the advent of Multi-Plants and my current methods of keeping plants growing on through winter I now feed all year long.

- Do not feed any plant that has become dry at the roots. The best treatment for a fuchsia that has wilted badly is to place it in a cool place out of sun, give the foliage an overhead spray, and only water the compost when the plant has revived.

- Although it is not a feed as such, seaweed extract is a marvellous tonic for plants. Use 'Maxicrop Original' at a rate of 10ml per gallon at every watering or whenever you feed (it can be safely mixed with all liquid feeds) your plants.

  Note: Since using 'Maxicrop Original' at every watering I have found that I have not had as much trouble with Whitefly. I have seen the odd Whitefly on my plants but have not seen any eggs on the leaves, so it may be that Maxicrop causes the sap to become obnoxious to them. Insects aren't fools, they won't lay their eggs on something that is not going to provide food for their young. I cannot say definitely that this product is a complete answer to the problem of Whitefly, but I can honestly say that I can find no other reason as to why they have stopped laying eggs on my plants!

Something that we haven't talked about whilst dealing with feeding is the gentle art of watering. There is one thing that is vital if we are to keep our pot grown fuchsias (any pot plant for that matter) healthy and that is to see that the roots have an ample supply of oxygen. You can make sure that a plant gets regular changes of air in the pot by allowing the compost to nearly dry out between each watering. Remember, allowing a plant to come close to a wilt before watering results in success. Keeping the compost permanently wet can lead to *DISASTER*.

Pests and Diseases

Fuchsias have such tender succulent leaves that it is not surprising they are a most attractive host for aphids, other sap sucking insects, and some diseases. I will begin this most important of chapters with the best advice that anyone can offer where pests and diseases are concerned.

PREVENTION IS BETTER THAN CURE

Anyone who grows fuchsias will have most of the following pests and diseases on their plants at one time or another. The main objective with any of them is early detection and preventative action to ensure that they don't become a major problem.

My main weapons against the enemy are my eyes. Whenever I handle a plant I am always on the lookout for the first signs of trouble. If I see the odd Greenfly or Whitefly I simply rub it out with finger and thumb. Similarly, the first sign of disease is dealt with immediately, not when it has got out of control. It is amazing how clean you can keep your plants by using these methods.

The task of keeping plants pest and disease free during the summer months is made much easier if they come into spring with clean, healthy growth. To achieve this I would suggest that you fumigate the greenhouse (if you have one) several times during winter and early spring. Changing over to a weekly spray of insecticide or fungicide, when the greenhouse is ventilated for spring and summer. These preventative sprays should be carried on until flowering time, then, because spray can mark flowers, revert to the finger and thumb method.

I will now describe the pests and diseases that attack fuchsias, and the methods that I use to control them.

Greenfly

You should be able to see at a glance if Greenfly are attacking your plants. There are two visible signs to look for: **a)** If there is a sticky substance on the leaves, check under the ones above and you will probably find Greenfly. **b)** Take note of the plant's own defence mechanism. If Greenfly are feeding on your fuchsias, the leaves under attack distort and curl. During the summer months Greenfly tend to go for flowers, so watch out for buds taking on a *BANANA* shape.

Methods of Control:

- If you notice them early enough they can be rubbed out with finger and thumb.
- By weekly sprays with a suitable insecticide.
- If you have an infestation, it is more effective to plunge the head of the plant (not when in flower) in a bucket of spray strength insecticide.

Whitefly

Whitefly are becoming an ever increasing problem, with even commercial growers having difficulty controlling them. Fortunately you are soon aware they are on your plants because they fly when disturbed. This early warning sign should tell you to take prompt action to prevent an infestation. The first thing that you need to know if you are going to control Whitefly is that they can, depending on the time of year, lay their eggs in as little as four or five days after hatching. With this pest it is no use spraying your plants at ten day or even weekly intervals as they will have laid their eggs long before your next spray. And as there are no insecticides available to the amateur that attack the eggs or scale stage of their life cycle, it is vital that you kill the adults before they have a chance to lay their eggs.

Methods of Control:

- The most successful method of control is to be constantly on the alert. Whenever I handle a plant I look under the leaves, if I see a Whitefly it is immediately squashed.
- Although they are almost immune, it will still pay to spray the plants at *THREE* day intervals with a range of suitable insecticides. Although it doesn't say so on the label, Liquid Derris (BIO) will kill the adult insects.
- When spraying, pay particular attention to the underside of the leaves.
- Please see the second note on page 83 for another product which may help to stop Whitefly becoming a problem.

Sciarid Fly

This insect is also called the Mushroom Fly because of its preference for peat as a breeding ground. They are about the size of a Midge and have a tendency to swarm when disturbed. Other than laying their eggs in the compost the adult fly does not seem to do any harm. The problem arises when the eggs hatch into tiny (about half an inch in length and looking very similar to a fine root) larvae which then feed on the roots of the plant.

Although I cannot say that I have ever lost a plant because of this insect, I have a friend who says that he has. The answer to the problem of Sciarid Fly is to kill the adults before they lay their eggs.

Methods of Control:

- Fumigate the greenhouse whenever necessary.
- You will kill a great many of these insects when spraying your plants for other pests if you also spray the greenhouse staging.
- Because the larvae are the main problem, sprinkle a little insect-powder on the surface of the compost or water the plant with a spray strength of a suitable insecticide.
- This is an insect that doesn't bother me too much. I see them around my plants but I have yet to see any plant damage.

Red Spider Mite

Red Spider is a pest that can easily get out of control. The main reason for this is that they are virtually impossible to see with the naked eye. Because they are so small it is usually only when a plant shows signs of infestation that you become aware of their presence.

The first sign of trouble will show on plants that have lost their glow of health, and have leaves that are unusually yellowing. Although leaves on the ripening wood of a fuchsia can naturally turn yellow, watch out for any showing a mottled effect. Remove any leaf that shows this fault and hold it up to the light, if Red Spider Mite is present you will be able to see through the areas where the insect has been feeding. With the aid of a magnifying glass you should be able to see the tiny mites moving about amidst their webs.

Methods of Control:

- Immediately isolate any plant that shows signs of infection as this insect is perhaps the hardest to eradicate.

- Using a powerful spray, blast a suitable insecticide through the webs to get at the pests.

- If only a few plants have become infected, and if you have other plants of those cultivars it may be safer, because Red Spider Mite is such a serious pest, to destroy them to prevent an infestation.

- There is one condition that may help deter Red Spider Mite, and that is to grow your plants in a humid atmosphere. It is said that they thrive in dry conditions, so you may well discourage them by keeping plenty of moisture around the plants.

Capsid Bug

This light green coloured insect (similar to a Greenfly in its early stages but grows to about ¼" in length as it matures) moves quickly when disturbed and is a pest not usually noticed until damage has been caused. If you see distorted growth and tiny black marks on the growing tips of a plant, be on the lookout for the Capsid Bug. This pest is more of a problem on garden plants, but if it does find its way into the greenhouse it can cause serious problems, with badly attacked plants not flowering at all that season.

Method of Control:

- Regularly spray for prevention using a suitable insecticide, as soon as the plants begin to come into full leaf.

Thrip

This is another insect that because of its size (minute) is difficult to see. Plant damage is usually the first sign of their presence.

Symptoms and treatment are similar to those given for Capsid Bug.

Note 1: I have noticed that damage caused by Thrip can show initially on a single plant, which can be quite seriously damaged, whilst others around it have not been touched. It seems possible that the insect could be overwintering on mature plants without being noticed. I would suggest that a spray or two with a suitable insecticide through the winter period would not be a bad idea.

Vine Weevil

Damage done by the nocturnal adult weevil is usually not too serious. The first signs that they have been feeding on the plant will be when you notice half moon shaped pieces eaten out of the edge of leaves. The main problem will occur when eggs, laid in the compost during summer, hatch out. The cream coloured grubs, which are similar in size to a bluebottle maggot, are easily recognisable as they have a brown head and are usually curled into a semi-circular shape. It is these grubs that cause the damage by feeding on the thick roots of older plants, with badly attacked plants ultimately dying. Soilless composts are favoured by the weevil, so be wary if you grow your plants in that type of compost.

It is difficult to tell when Vine Weevil grubs are present because they live out of sight in the compost. My method of detecting them starts in autumn and continues throughout the winter months. I check each plant to see that it is firmly anchored in the compost and that the surface of the compost has not been disturbed. If I find one that is loose, or the top of the rootball shows signs of tiny *wormcasts* (usually close to the stem of the plant), I remove it from its pot to inspect the rootball for any sign of the grubs. On plants where they are present I remove as much of the compost as possible, paying particular attention to the thick roots at the crown of the plant, to make sure that I remove them all. The plant is then repotted into a pot that will comfortably take the roots (usually a smaller one) using fresh compost. After watering the plant carefully (not too wet) it is placed in shady position where, hopefully, it will recover.

Methods of Control:

- Use a compost that contains grit to help deter the adult weevil from laying its eggs.
- Firm your compost if you use John Innes type composts, or if your soilless compost contains perlite and grit.
- Mix a little insect-powder containing gamma HCH into your potting compost.

- Drench the rootball with a spray strength of insecticide (see page 94). This treatment should be done periodically during July, August and September. Do *NOT* drench plants in the cold months of the year.

- In summer, if you have noticed Vine Weevil damage to the foliage, visit the greenhouse after dark when you may well see them feeding. They are dark brown in colour with yellowish speckles on their back, wingless, have a very hard shell, and being slow moving are easily picked off the plant and destroyed.

- In the daytime they hide in all sorts of places, look for them under the pot, behind the label, in fact anywhere that is out of sight.

- See page 29 for another point of view on this problem pest.

Western Flower Thrip

This insect attacks a wide range of plants and because of its life cycle is a most difficult pest to control. The Western Flower Thrip is minute in size, elongated in shape and can vary in colour. The eggs, after being laid on the plant, hatch, then develop into a nymph stage. They then drop onto and live in the compost for a few days before emerging again as mature insects. Because they are so small the first sign that you have of this pest will probably be when you notice damage to your plants. The Western Flower Thrip, as its name implies, feeds on the flowers of the plant (entering at the bud stage), and in the flowering season this will be its first port of call. Earlier in the season, however, it will also attack the growing shoots of plants causing them to become distorted. As this stage can take ten days or more to show it is important that you recognise the symptoms at the earliest, and start an immediate spraying programme.

Methods of Control:

- Like most pests and diseases, Western Flower Thrip will be brought into contact with your fuchsias on infected new stock. Isolate any plants that you buy, or are given, until you are sure they are clean.

- Inspect your plants frequently. If you notice unusual damage *(distortion)* to flowers or growing shoots, be on the safe side and treat as for Western Flower Thrip.

- It is important that you keep hitting them hard at *THREE* day intervals with at least three different insecticides that will kill Thrips until all your plants are clean again.
- As part of their life cycle is in the compost it may help if you dust the surface with an insect-powder, or drench the rootball with a spray strength of insecticide.

Caterpillars

Caterpillars are the bane of my life, they come in all shapes and sizes to attack my plants. Some are so tiny that they aren't noticed until you see that something has eaten away the top surface of the leaf, whilst others are so large (the Elephant Hawk Moth caterpillar) that you almost see plants disappear before your eyes. Let me tell you about my *favourite*! In summer, you may see large dark brown moths in your greenhouse. These sneaky creatures intrigue me as they usually lay only one egg on a plant.

The first sign of trouble is something that looks like mouse dirt on a leaf, on closer inspection you may see a tiny hole in a flower bud or leaves that are being nibbled away. Now! Find the caterpillar. You know there is one on the plant somewhere, but where? I have even found these masters of camouflage lying length ways down the stem between leaf axils. Search until you find it, however, because they can cause a great deal of damage. Shaking the plant when the caterpillars are small sometimes dislodges them, but as they get older they hang on like grim death.

Methods of Control:
- Find and remove the caterpillars.
- Spray with a suitable insecticide.
- The best defence is to cover the open windows and door with plastic mesh netting to keep the butterflies and moths out.

Bees and Wasps

Both these insects should be kept out of the greenhouse.

Bees can cause a great deal of damage to flowers as they lumber about in search of pollen, badly marking the corolla as they grip the petals with their enormous feet.

Wasps are even worse as they are inclined to bore holes through the sepals and corolla to get directly to their objective, they can also further mutilate the flowers by chewing off the anthers and stigma.

Botrytis

This terrible disease, commonly known as *GREY MOULD*, can be quite devastating if it is allowed to get out of control. Spraying and fumigation may help to clean up an attack, but the main objective with Botrytis is to make sure that the greenhouse conditions are not in its favour. Again, prevention is better than cure, Botrytis thrives in a cool, close, humid atmosphere, and usually starts on damaged or dead plant material.

Methods of Control:

- Ventilate the greenhouse whenever possible, even in winter and early spring, to ensure good air circulation around the plants.

- Do not have too much moisture lying about during the cold, damp periods of the year.

- Remove yellowing, damaged or dead leaves from plants, compost surface or greenhouse staging when doing your weekly inspection.

- Some cultivars, because of their tendency to have an over abundance of foliage, are more prone than others to Botrytis. This heavy covering of leaves can prevent the flow of air through the plant, causing leaves or even branches to be attacked. Your first sign of trouble will be the loss of fresh green leaves. To help prevent this happening, remove some of the leaves from the centre of the plant so that air can circulate.

- Botrytis can also creep up the main stem on young plants. You will recognise this by leaves falling off the stem while they are still green. The stem will also become discoloured and covered with tiny hairs. As this type of Botrytis usually comes from below soil level, it could have been caused by damage to the stem when the plant was taken as a cutting. I always use a knife of almost razor blade sharpness when propagating. The cleaner the cut, the quicker it will heal and form a callus, and the less chance there will be of infection.

- The initial growth on plants brought through winter in a dormant or semi-dormant state can also suffer from Botrytis. If you look carefully at where the disease has started you will usually find that it is around the end of a cut stem. You will also notice that the diseased leaves have been in contact with sap exuding from these cut ends, and it is this that causes the problem. The action I take once I notice leaves have been damaged by Botrytis is simply to rub out, with finger and thumb, the infected area and try and make sure other leaves are kept away from problem areas.

• I do not use fungicides to combat Botrytis — my own preventative action is to have plenty of air circulating around and through the plants.

Root Rot

This disease is usually brought on by a cultural fault, overwatering or overfeeding. Some cultivars require less water than others, but it is very easy in summer to neglect this fact and water every plant whether it needs it or not. This, in my experience, is when Root Rot starts to develop. I try and make sure that any cultivar that tends to suffer from this fault is allowed to nearly dry out before rewatering.

• The first signs of anything going wrong with the root of a plant will show on the foliage. Any plant on which the leaves suddenly lose their sheen should have its roots examined. Remove it from its pot and if the roots do not look a healthy white or brownish colour (if Root Rot has occurred they will be black) suspect that the plant has a root problem.

• To try and rescue a plant where the root has been damaged by rot it is imperative that feeding is stopped immediately and water only given when the compost is on the point of drying out. Then keep the plant in a shady place until, hopefully the leaves start to brighten up again.

Fuchsia Rust

This disease is aptly named because the small patches of orange postules that are to be found on the underside of leaves, look similar to rust on metal. Although this disease is an airborne one I find that it is invariably brought in on fresh stock. With Rust, great care must be taken. It is imperative that you notice it in its early stages, otherwise you could have a catastrophe on your hands. If you see small dark patches on the surface of the leaves, look underneath. If you see the postules described above immediately isolate the plant and start a rigorous inspection programme to prevent the infection spreading.

Methods of Control:

- Carefully remove and destroy infected leaves. Do this well away from other plants as the spores are easily spread.
- Regularly spray infected plants with a suitable fungicide.
- Inspect the plants every two or three days to make certain that the disease has not spread.
- Once you have had Rust keep a careful watch each spring and autumn, it can easily return.

Scorch

The symptoms of Scorch (usually on plants under glass) are brown patches that go right through the leaf. This is not a disease, it is a cultural fault caused by spraying the foliage with water on sunny days. Droplets of water then act like a magnifying glass causing the sun to burn the tissue of the leaves. The solution to this problem is either to use more shading on the glass or not to spray the plants on sunny days.

Note: I do not recommend spraying water over plants to create humidity as it can cause problems. Plants can be damaged by Botrytis or scorched by the sun dependent on the prevailing conditions. Humidity should be provided by moistening the area surrounding the plants — see page 3.

Sooty Mould

This black fungal growth can make fuchsias look unsightly. Sooty Mould will appear on the foliage of your plants only if they have become infested with aphids, or something similar — it grows on the sticky substance secreted by the insects. The answer to this problem is simple. Do not allow the plants to become infested.

Now for some advice on the subject of spraying:

- Use a sprayer with a fine mist as large droplets of some insecticides can burn tender new shoots.

- Use several different insecticides in rotation to prevent pests becoming immune.

- Do not be tempted to mix fungicides and insecticides together unless the manufacturer states that they can be safely mixed. To do so could cause possible damage, not only to the plants but also to yourself.

- Do not spray in sunny conditions.

- Take care when using chemicals. Always use protective gloves and a face mask.

- Always wash off any fungicide or insecticide immediately if any has inadvertently come in contact with your skin. This is *MOST* important.

Finally: There are two insecticides that I use and find effective on most pests, they are: **a)** 'Liquid Derris' (BIO) — This one, although it is not mentioned on the label, is also quite good with adult Whitefly. b) 'Sybol' (ZENACA) is the one I have also used as a drench to combat Vine Weevil grubs (see page 89). I deal with the two main diseases, Botrytis and Rust, in different ways: **a)** I find that Botrytis can be controlled simply be creating the correct growing conditions (see chapter one). **b)** Rust, on the other hand, is not quite as easily dealt with but I have found that 'Systhane' (PBI), which is actually made to combat Rust on roses is also very effective on fuchsias (I spray three times at three day intervals).

Note: In case of unavailability of the above named products, try anything that is new to you on only a few plants until you are happy that it does its job without damaging the plants.

I have no preference as to which insect-powder to use as I cannot remember when I last had need of one, but if I did have a need I would look out for one that contained 'gamma HCH' or any recommended substitute.

Triphylla Type Fuchsias

At least one of these fuchsia cultivars with their dark green leaves and contrasting long tubed orange flowers should be in everyone's collection, they really are striking. Triphylla type fuchsias are usually fairly strong growers and are an ideal plant for bedding out (for the summer months only) in the garden. However, they are not the easiest fuchsia to grow into a nice shaped pot plant, the reason being that they are invariably long jointed, are stiff vertical growers, and have a tendency to drop their lower leaves as growth ripens. The traditional 'grow-one-plant-in-a-pot' *rule* has led to a variety of methods being developed to overcome the above problems: **a)** The use of a long cutting so that quite a few leaf nodes are buried — this, to encourage as many shoots as possible to develop from below compost level. **b)** Pruning back quite hard each autumn to encourage more shoots to emerge from the base of the plant. **c)** The cutting off of quite a large portion of the rootball each spring and sinking the plant down (some growers even completely bury the entire plant) into a larger pot — this to cover much of the bare lower branches and to encourage even more new growth to emerge from below compost level.

To my mind the above methods, although they eventually produce a nice plant, mean that it has taken quite a few years to do so and perhaps also produced a plant far larger than most of us can manage. In fact these, and other methods devised, have been evolved to camouflage defects that can be overcome in the first place if we bring triphylla growing into the Multi-Plant age. But before we start discussing the benefits of using this method for growing triphyllas let me give you a short list of cultivars:

Bornemann's Beste; Brighton Belle; Coralle; Golden Arrow;

Gartenmeister Bonstedt; Leverkusen; Mary; Mantilla; Thalia; Trumpeter.

Now, let me describe the methods I have devised to turn these tall growing long jointed plants into beautifully shaped, reasonably compact pot plants:

- The cuttings I use, even though we are dealing with a large leafed plant are still the tiny soft growing tips of the shoots with most of the leaf area removed. The prepared cuttings are rooted either directly into the pot or in my alternative summer method of propagation, Perlite and Water, and if the latter they are then pricked out into the pot. I usually start my triphyllas off with a minimum of 10 cuttings in a 3½" pot. You may think that this is too many but my reasoning says, the less side shoots you get from a plant, the more plants you use. Once they are rooted and growing on I pinch them out quite early, probably at one or two sets of leaves — again, this is to produce as many sideshoots low down on the plant as possible. Then, as the plant grows, I pinch out at each set of leaves until I have built up a nice sized head with plenty of shoots, at which stage I then let it run to flower.

Note 1: When pinching out, bare in mind that triphyllas take 13 weeks or more from the last stop to the time they come into flower.

Note 2: I know that you will already be questioning my mentality in growing all those triphylla plants in a pot, but once you get into multi-planting you will find as I have that many plants in a pot grow in an entirely different way to a single plant. Just accept that this is an improved way of growing them and enjoy the wonderful results.

I almost always start them off in 3½" pots because it allows me, whilst they are still young, to lean outwards the outer ring of plants at each potting on stage, i.e. 3½" to 4¼" — 4¼" to 5", etc. This leaning out of plants removes what is perhaps the worst feature of triphyllas as they get older and that is their tendency to show a lot of bare stems at the base of the plant. And whilst we are at this early stage of their life don't forget the stroking down of foliage and the teasing out of sideshoots as described in the chapters on Multi-Plants and Bushes.

I would also suggest that you do not overpot triphyllas in their first year. The temptation, because they are such vigorous growers, is to keep potting them on until they are in quite a large pot. I think that this is a mistake and that you will find that containing them in perhaps a 5" pot for their first season helps to keep them more compact — without losing any quality of growth. As an example, I rooted 10 cuttings of Bornemann's Beste in a 4¼" pot on the 7th of March. Grew them on, with only one pinch out, and flowered them in the same pot. The plant grew into a beautiful shape and came into flower in time for me to take it to a talk in Anglesey in early September. The plant is still in flower now as I write these words on the 8th of December. I will lightly cut it back when it has finished flowering and pot it straight up into a 5" then, when ready, into a 6" pot to give me a larger plant next year. And unless I want an extremely large plant I will not take it through another winter I will simply repeat the process again.

Ken Pilkington,
33 Beckdean Avenue,
Poulton-le-Fylde,
Lancashire.
FY6 8BG
01253 886241

Dear Reader,

I hope that you have enjoyed my book, you may not have learnt where fuchsias originated or even who first found them, but if it has helped in any way to improve some aspect of your culture I will be well pleased.

To continue your interest in fuchsias why not join the British Fuchsia Society. For the cost of your membership fee you will receive an Annual Year Book, Bulletins in spring and autumn, and occasional other publications. You will also, for the cost of postage, receive three free rooted young plants, or advice on your fuchsia problems.

For more information, or if you wish to obtain further copies of this book, please contact me (enclosing a stamped addressed envelope) at the above address.

Kind Regards,

Ken